The Heart of Your Script

The Heart of Your Script

*The Insider's Guide to Writing the
Difficult Middle Section of a Screenplay*

Phil Hughes and Ted Wilkes

THE BRITISH FILM INSTITUTE

Bloomsbury Publishing Plc, 50 Bedford Square, London, WC1B 3DP, UK
Bloomsbury Publishing Inc, 1359 Broadway, New York, NY 10018, USA
Bloomsbury Publishing Ireland, 29 Earlsfort Terrace, Dublin 2, D02 AY28, Ireland

BLOOMSBURY is a trademark of Bloomsbury Publishing Plc

First published in Great Britain 2026 by Bloomsbury
on behalf of the
British Film Institute
21 Stephen Street, London W1T 1LN
www.bfi.org.uk

The BFI is the lead organization for film in the UK and the distributor of Lottery funds for film. Our mission is to ensure that film is central to our cultural life, in particular by supporting and nurturing the next generation of filmmakers and audiences. We serve a public role which covers the cultural, creative and economic aspects of film in the UK.

Copyright © Phil Hughes and Ted Wilkes, 2026

Phil Hughes and Ted Wilkes have asserted their right under the Copyright, Designs and Patents Act, 1988, to be identified as author of this work.

For legal purposes the Acknowledgements on p. ix constitute an extension of this copyright page.

Cover design: Louise Dugdale
Image figures: Phil Hughes

All rights reserved. No part of this publication may be: i) reproduced or transmitted in any form, electronic or mechanical, including photocopying, recording or by means of any information storage or retrieval system without prior permission in writing from the publishers; or ii) used or reproduced in any way for the training, development or operation of artificial intelligence (AI) technologies, including generative AI technologies. The rights holders expressly reserve this publication from the text and data mining exception as per Article 4(3) of the Digital Single Market Directive (EU) 2019/790.

Bloomsbury Publishing Plc does not have any control over, or responsibility for, any third-party websites referred to or in this book. All internet addresses given in this book were correct at the time of going to press. The author and publisher regret any inconvenience caused if addresses have changed or sites have ceased to exist, but can accept no responsibility for any such changes.

A catalogue record for this book is available from the British Library.

A catalog record for this book is available from the Library of Congress.

ISBN:	HB:	978-1-8390-2811-3
	PB:	978-1-8390-2810-6
	ePDF:	978-1-8390-2813-7
	eBook:	978-1-8390-2812-0

Typeset by Integra Software Services Pvt. Ltd.
Printed and bound in India

For product safety related questions contact productsafety@bloomsbury.com.

To find out more about our authors and books visit www.bloomsbury.com and sign up for our newsletters.

Phil Hughes
For Sarah. For her love, understanding and encouragement. Also for Franny, Freya and Xanthe who make our lives so much better.

Ted Wilkes
For Marlow. You weren't born when I started writing this, but I already had so many stories I couldn't wait to tell you.

Contents

List of illustrations viii
Acknowledgements ix
Introduction x

1. The mechanics 1
2. Willing 19
3. Unknowing 35
4. Unable to believe 49
5. Accidental 63
6. Mistaken 79
7. Willing case study: *Inside Out 2* (2024) 93
8. Unknowing case study: *The Fall Guy* (2024) 107
9. Unable-to-believe case study: *Barbie* (2023) 121
10. Accidental case study: *Everything Everywhere All at Once* (2022) 135
11. Mistaken case study: *Talk to Me* (2023) 149
12. Character Is Structure does TV 161

Index 172

Illustrations

1 *The path, where all great stories begin* 1
2 *Your willing chosen one must find a key to unlock their story* 19
3 *Your unknowing chosen one will have to negotiate two gates to navigate their journey* 35
4 *The unable to believe chosen one must come to appreciate the armour they have* 49
5 *The heart of every story lies off the path, nowhere is this truer than with the accidental chosen one* 63
6 *The most terrifying of wolves stalk our mistaken chosen ones … or they end up becoming one* 79

Acknowledgements

When we finished our last book, we still had so many ideas that we wanted to develop and pass on to screenwriters. Further exploring the tricky central two-thirds of a narrative arc seemed like the perfect place to continue our explorations into storytelling as there is so little written that explicitly tackles this incredibly important and difficult part of the writing process. We would like to thank Anna Coatman and Barbara Cohen Bastos, our tireless editors at Bloomsbury, who assisted us in developing the manuscript into the shape that you now find it. We would like to thank the reviewers of the initial text for their time and honest critique that informed the changes we made to the piece. A special thanks must go to the Canonbury Tavern which became a remote outpost for us to discuss pages and eventually chapters that we had written. A fictionalized account of one of those meetings graces the cover of this book. We would be remiss for not again thanking Chris and Bob at the London Screenwriters' Festival who have given us a platform over the past few years to explore our work with a host of emerging screenwriters both online and in person. Again, we must thank our friends, families and colleagues for enduring our insistent interruptions of the films (and now TV shows) they are trying to watch so we can point out the underlying mechanics of the narratives they merely hoped to be absorbed in. We promise that we might stop doing it one day. Finally, a big thank you to the students that we teach at our present and past institutions for embracing the ideas that we explore with them in class. The greatest pleasure of our profession is assisting someone to discover the thing that it is they want to tell stories about and shape an initial idea into a compelling narrative for the screen.

Introduction

Welcome to our second book on effective storytelling for the screen. If you have read our first, *Character Is Structure: The Insider's Guide to Screenwriting*, you will be familiar with the central thesis of our work on the development of the effective screenplay. To recap, when you are developing a storyline, you will discover that there are only four essential story pathways acting as an invitation for your central character, or chosen one, to enter into your story. There is also a fifth inversion of these paths, the path trodden by the anti-hero. Don't worry if you haven't read that book (yet), as we will be reminding you of the paradigms, and you can always investigate those ideas in more detail after you've thoroughly enjoyed this current work.

In our first book, we concentrated on outlining ways into your screenplay. This is the moment that we call the invitation: the invitation that your chosen one must receive and respond to in order to enter into your dark forest. Each invitation, we suggest, comes with its own last-throw-of-the-dice moment which will see your chosen one exit the dark forest or not exit the dark forest, depending on your chosen pathway. These obligatory actions, we would argue, allow for your chosen one to experience the greatest amount of growth and change during their journey through the dark forest. Furthermore, these trajectories that we set our chosen ones on allow for the most profound emotional and dramaturgical engagement with the ideas you have decided to explore. This then feeds into the reaction an audience will have to watching, or reading, your work. Effectively structuring your work at these key moments allows for a more satisfying engagement with the words you have written on the page. We also looked at the events at the midpoint of your screenplay and proposed a number of different elements which go to make up a successful midpoint, adding to the dramatic impetus to take your characters through the remainder of your story.

Now that we've dealt with the beginning and the end of your story, in this book, as the title suggests, we will be looking at the heart of the screenplay; those central fifty to sixty pages of a standard-length film script which so many writers find difficult to negotiate. We both read and write screenplays for a living, and, apart from our own storytelling struggles, we see many of the same issues arising with screenplays again and again, one of the most familiar of which is the inability of the writer to sustain the drama through the central section of the script. This is what we will be helping you with in the following pages.

The central two-thirds of any narrative is the much-discussed thorn in the writer's side. Many a screenplay is abandoned during this stretch of the story, either because there isn't enough in the idea or there's too much to fit into it. With nothing else for it the piece is simply pushed into a drawer (or hard drive) somewhere and forgotten. With this book we hope to be the signpost in your own dark forest as we help you with fashioning your idea into a workable and marketable screenplay to be proud of.

We are going to begin our journey into the heart of the script by proposing a universal storytelling rule: at the heart of all good stories there is a single question. For example:

- Will a man be able to save the galaxy? (*Star Wars: Episode IV – A New Hope*)
- Can a girl get home after being swept away by a tornado? (*The Wizard of Oz*)
- Will a woman be able to catch a serial killer? (*The Silence of the Lambs*)
- Can a group of teenagers survive being attacked by a knife-wielding maniac? (*Scream*)
- Will a group of men be able to defend a village from bandits? (*Seven Samurai*)

This central question, which you must have in your script if your storytelling is to be successful, not only drives and motivates the central ideas within the narrative but also informs all of the scenes and sequences that you are writing. Often writing can feel like it lacks focus when there are scenes and sequences that stray too far away from exploring the central question that you have initially proposed within your opening acts.

You must identify this central question as soon as you are able to as you begin to develop your screenplay and remain true to this question throughout. As we have considered this idea in the writing of this book, we have concluded that the successful, well-written screenplay forms itself around a simple narrative. A single question running through the script that everything else hangs off creates a focused, dramatic storyline that is easy for your audience to follow and engage with. However, we are not all seeking to write fairy stories or simplistic children's stories. We want to build complex worlds and explore the depths of the human psyche, don't we? This does not require us to write more convoluted stories. It does, however, require us to write more complex characters. The first rule of any successful screenplay and the major focus of the overarching narrative of your screenplay, then, is: simple story, complex character. Write it on a Post-it note and stick it on your computer screen. If you crack this one then you are on the way to writing a screenplay that will be telling the story you want to tell in the way you want to tell it because it is the complexity of the character that makes the simple question at the heart of your screenplay so difficult to answer and allows for your unique voice to come through on the page.

Simple story, complex character

As we explore this notion, let's take that initial question posed at the centre of *Star Wars: Episode IV – A New Hope*:

Will a man be able to save the galaxy?

From what? Why? How equipped or not equipped is he to do the task? Currently, there is no real heart to the story that couldn't be found in another generic space opera. We know that there is an ambiguous beginning (there is a man) and an ending (save the galaxy). However, it lacks an understanding of what will happen within the central two-thirds of the narrative. Let's begin to build it out.

> A princess sends a message to the man she thinks will be able to save her and the galaxy.

This is getting better. There is an expectation to our chosen one's action(s) now. He is being relied on not just to save the galaxy but also to save the princess. We have a macro conflict and a micro conflict to the narrative that we are going to be able to explore within the heart of the narrative. However, we can still do better.

> When a princess in distress sends a message to a young farmhand, he must leave his home planet where he has spent his entire life and save the galaxy.

Better still. We now understand more about the situation that the princess is in with the opening clause and a clearer picture of how equipped the man is to take on the challenge(s) in front of him. He will have a long journey to go on if he is going to become the saviour of the galaxy.

> When a princess in distress sends a message to her estranged brother, a young farmhand who has never left his home planet, he must decide if he will accept the challenge to become a Jedi knight and save the galaxy.

Now we're getting more into the heart of the story. It's become very clear that we are firmly in space-opera territory now. We're not quite sure what a Jedi knight is without greater context, but that's fine at this point because currently it gives a clear sense of the trajectory that he will go on (farmhand to knight). In addition, we are giving our man some agency in allowing him a choice in the matter. However, the best part is that we are introduced to the family dynamics, hinting at the complexity of the characters who will be navigating through this 'simple' plot.

> When a princess in distress sends a message to her estranged brother, a young farmhand who has never left his home planet, he must decide if he will accept the challenge to train as a Jedi knight and save the galaxy from the clutches of the evil Darth Vader who is also his father.

We could continue until we have built out something akin to a synopsis or a treatment for this idea as this single-sentence summary is getting slightly unwieldy now. However, in this final iteration of the idea, we are given the clearest picture yet of the micro and the macro conflict(s) that we will see during the piece. We now have the basis of a simple story and a complex character from which the rest of the screenplay will grow.

This notion of *Simple story, complex character* will resonate throughout this book, and you will see the importance of grasping this formula if you want to write a successful script. If the question at the heart of your screenplay is fuzzy or unfocused, then your scenes and sequences will begin to fragment and fall apart with nothing solid to cohere around.

In script development, you will be asked questions such as, 'What is this scene doing for us?', 'How is this scene advancing the central question?', 'Is this something that is helping us?' Scenes that move into exploring issues that do not support the central question that you are exploring distract from the journey you are taking us on. Staying with the Star Wars franchise for a minute, we could do worse than look at the extended pod-racing sequence in *Star Wars: Episode I – The Phantom Menace* (1999) for an example of a sequence, however spectacular, that does little to push the drama forward and answer the central question of the film: 'Will a young slave with dark tendencies be accepted into the Jedi order?'

Momentum and stakes are always your best friends when crafting the mid-section of a narrative. Anything that feels like it is not deliberately slowing the pace of a piece down for clear dramatic purposes gives the audience the opportunity to disengage from the drama, and you have then lost them. There are ebbs and flows to all screenplays, but knowing when these need to come within a narrative is a skill that comes from understanding the craft of writing and identifying the single, simple dramatic question at the heart of your story.

One of the tools that we used in the first book, and which we will return to here, is the fairy or folk tale. We find these universally known and understood stories are useful in helping us to understand effective storytelling. Many of these stories are so embedded into our psyches that they must be doing something right.

We noticed early on in our dissection of the fairy story, when preparing for our first book, that many of these tales have passive protagonists or protagonists who aren't really the protagonists at all. Sleeping Beauty is really the story of a handsome prince discovering the truth about a legendary slumbering princess in the forest. Cinderella is surely the tale of a handsome prince desperately searching for his lost love with only a glass slipper for a clue. Rapunzel tells of a handsome prince who saves a young woman with very long hair trapped in a tower. The handsome princes are the heroes who take action and affect the outcomes of the stories, but they have very little in the way of personality. They are not interesting characters. The stories are named after the interesting characters who find themselves in trouble but do little, independently, to get themselves out of it. Protagonists have to take action in order for stories to work. We all know that, right? Surely then, Sleeping Beauty, Cinderella and Rapunzel are the wrong protagonists – at least from the point of view of the screenplay writer. If we were writing these stories today, we would presumably be spending our time on creating handsome princes with complex characters, fascinating back stories and solid wants and needs, or following Disney's lead and keeping the bland handsome princes but working on the complexities of the princesses involved.

For the purposes of our foray into the middle section of your screenplays and our exploration of the simple story inhabited by the complex character, we are going to use one of these stories with the wrong protagonist and reinvent it in various ways in order to investigate how you can make the most of your dramas over the length of a feature film.

Little Red Riding Hood is the story of a young girl who is threatened by a grandma-eating wolf before her life is saved by a huntsman. Obviously, the huntsman takes all the action in this story, but there is nothing particularly interesting about him. The question at the heart of the story is straightforward: 'Will a little girl survive a trip through the woods to her sick grandmother's house?'

Little Red Riding Hood, herself, is not a complex character in the fairy story, and neither is the real protagonist of the story, the huntsman, but we can work on that. It is in her interactions with the wolf in the forest that we can first identify potential for the story to be derailed by scenes that detract from the central question.

The wolf approaches Little Red Riding Hood and asks her what is in her basket. We don't care what is in her basket. The wolf doesn't care what is in her basket. A lesser writer with a hundred pages of screenplay to fill might spend some time on exploring the contents of Little Red Riding Hood's basket, but in the lean, focused fairy story we are all familiar with we realize very quickly that the wolf's question is only a way of gaining Little Red Riding Hood's trust so that he can ask her the question he really wants to ask: 'Where does Grandma live?' The slight detour into the question about the contents of the basket are a means to an end for the wolf, and the story remains focused on the central question of Little Red Riding Hood's dangerous trip through the forest.

We refer to these moments in screenplays where blind alleys, dead scenes and pointless forays into the unknown exist as 'Basket Scenes'. Beware the basket scene as you progress through your screenplay. Focus on the single question and concentrate on the complex character. If tangential questions creep in, make sure that they are actually a subset of the central and only question you are asking in your script.

Little Red Riding Hood is an ancient tale handed down via oral tradition, but there are two authoritative written versions of this story. The first was penned by Charles Perrault in the 1690s and as a warning to children not to walk through the woods without taking due care and attention, and it ends with Little Red Riding Hood getting eaten by the wolf. The wolf, by the way, has already eaten the grandma. Quite the warning. In the second version, published over a hundred years later, the story was appropriated by the Brothers Grimm, who added the huntsman who at the end saves the day. For the purposes of this book, we are going to be using the milder, Grimm Brothers version. At least it adds a final act, even if it is a bit deus ex machina.

So, we will be putting Little Red Riding Hood to work in exploring our story pathways and our essential chosen ones, and Little Red Riding Hood will also be encountering a number of different elements which will take various forms depending on the pathway we send her on. These tools appear universally at the heart of all screenplays and are easy to understand, but they manifest themselves differently depending on the nature of the chosen one and the pathway that they are on.

Before we begin, we are going to recap our story pathways in brief. If you want to explore these in more detail (and we recommend that you do) then you can refer back to our first book, but in order to place the following ideas in context it is useful for us to at least give you, or remind you, of an overview of the pathways.

The willing chosen one

This chosen one enters your story voluntarily. They decide to participate in your narrative following a clear invitation which they barely hesitate over before accepting. They are the most heroic of all chosen ones and believe themselves to be equipped for the task in front of them. The task, however, will be somewhat more difficult than they imagined and, following their time in the dark forest, they will realize that this is an inherently negative space and that they must burn the forest in order to emerge as a hero at the end.

Examples: Aatami Korpi (*Sisu* 2022), Gus March-Phillips (*The Ministry of Ungentlemanly Warfare* 2024), *One Life* (1930s plotline) (2023).

The unknowing chosen one

The unknowing chosen one finds themselves participating in your story against their better judgement. Their once upon a time is upset by the intervention of a disruptor who will lead them away from their normal lives and do a deal with them to complete what appears to be a relatively simple task. The task, however, will be nothing of the sort, and the deal will be an uneven bargain; to leave the story, the unknowing chosen one must arrange for the deal to be undone.

Examples: *The Instigators* (2024), *Dune: Part Two* (2024), *The Whale* (2022)

The unable-to-believe chosen one

This character is an ugly duckling who has no sense of their own worth. They do not wish to participate in your story and will need a mentor or tormentor to pull them through the narrative where they will eventually emerge as they become a swan.

Examples: *One Life* (1980s plotline) (2023), *The Holdovers* (2023), *Guardians of the Galaxy Vol. 2* (2017)

The accidental chosen one

The accidental chosen one finds themselves thrust into your story unwillingly and unknowingly. They are plucked from their once upon a time and spend the narrative attempting to get back home. During the course of their adventures, they will learn some essential truths about themselves which will allow them to experience the return.

Examples: *The End We Start From* (2023), *Land of Bad* (2024), *The Quiet Girl* (2022)

The mistaken chosen one

This final pathway represents the journey trodden by the anti-hero. These mistaken chosen ones believe that they are on one of the preceding four pathways, but they are not. Mistaken/willing chosen ones may decide they like the dark forest too much and, rather than burning it down, may decide to remain and reign over the space. Mistaken/unknowing chosen ones embrace the uneven bargain and find themselves unable or unwilling to undo that deal. Mistaken/unable to believe chosen ones search in vain for mentors to help them become the swans they so long to be; consequently they will always be ugly ducklings in these stories. Mistaken/accidental chosen ones find themselves in the darkest of dark forests often being chased by monsters or crazed killers. More often than not, they will never experience any return to normality.

Examples: Mistaken/willing: Edith Swan (*Wicked Little Letters*, 2023); mistaken/unknowing: Oliver Quick (*Saltburn*, 2023); mistaken/unable to believe: Owen (*I Saw the TV Glow*, 2024); mistaken/accidental: Beth (*Evil Dead Rise*, 2023)

Acts

We are almost ready to set off on our first journey with Little Red Riding Hood, but, before that, a brief note about acts. As with our first book we will be using the five-act model which allows us to dissect the screenplay into clear movements and isolate the central acts and their intent in our exploration of the heart of the screenplay.

Act 1 shows us your chosen one's once upon a time. Here we meet the main characters who inhabit the world of the chosen one and see that world before it is changed by the events that are to come. This act generally includes an inciting incident – something that happens to hint at a major change to come.

In Act 2, an invitation is accepted by the chosen one. This invitation may have been issued in Act 1 or during this act, but it is the chosen one's reaction to the invitation that determines which pathway they are on and how they will enter the dark forest.

Act 3 shows the chosen one's foray into the dark forest. Here they begin to explore the world they have been thrust into, far from their once upon a time. This act is split by the midpoint of the film and represents two sides to the tale, which often mirror one another. After the midpoint, Act 3 continues to show us the dark forest, but your chosen one is now deeper in and finding it more difficult to find a way out.

In Act 4, your chosen one must gather up all of their wits in an attempt to leave the dark forest. Here all appears lost but there is a glimmer of hope in the last-throw-of-the-dice moment before, in Act 5 they experience their (un)happily ever after.

The essential elements of Acts 2, 3 and 4

In this book, we will be concentrating on the journey through the dark forest following your chosen one's acceptance of the invitation and culminating in their last-throw-of-the-dice moment. We have identified six essential elements that a successful central section of a screenplay will include and, over the course of these pages, we will be revealing how effective, versatile and necessary these elements are. They are useful tools that you will be able to deploy throughout your narrative in order to maintain the drama, up the stakes, build greater and more interesting obstacles and challenge your chosen one's conflicted nature.

The first element around which so much of the action of your screenplay will coalesce is the path.

The path

The chosen one will set off on their journey into the dark forest and the path that they decide to take will lead them to the end of the dark forest. The end of your story. The final act of your film. Waiting at the end of the path will be the gate.

The gate

This is the way out of your story for your chosen one. The gate stands, or appears to stand, at the end of the path with the promise of a return to the chosen one's once upon a time, but in order to get through the gate your chosen one is going to need the key.

The key

Depending on the nature of your story, this may be many different things but it will always be difficult, and sometimes impossible, to find. Your chosen one will need the key to unlock the gate to allow them to leave your film (something that most chosen ones are desperate to do), but some chosen ones never find the key, or decide not to use it. You will only discover this when you allow your chosen one to explore off the path.

Off the path

It is away from the main path that your chosen one will truly experience your story. Here they will learn and grow, gathering experience to allow them to complete the tasks in front of them, because, hidden in the dark forest there will be the wolf.

The wolf

There may be more than one wolf, and the wolf may have many disguises, but there will definitely be an antagonist out there that your chosen one will have to confront as they journey through the dark forest. How they deal with the wolf may be somewhat dependent upon the skills that they bring with them into that place in the form of the suit of armour.

The suit of armour

This element of your story has many different roles. It may help your chosen one in their battles by protecting them. It may hold them back due its weight and cumbersome nature. It may change in form and effectiveness through the course of the narrative. The suit of armour is an intrinsic part of the chosen one's make-up as they enter the heart of your narrative, and you should pay careful attention as to its form and effectiveness.

This all sounds pretty straightforward so far, right? These elements are easy to understand and useful to deploy in your storytelling, but there is one more factor you need to understand as we explore these ideas in more detail: while these elements appear in one form or another in every well told story, each of our different pathways comes with an extra element that is unique to that pathway. So, the selection and identification of your pathway is vital in the development of your story. We will expand upon each of these as we move forward, but, in brief, the elements particular to each pathway are:

- Willing: the match
- Unknowing: the first gate
- Unable to believe: the mentor/tormentor
- Accidental: the gatekeeper

The heart of Little Red Riding Hood according to the Brothers Grimm

As an exercise, let us take a look at the version of Little Red Riding Hood that we are all familiar with and apply these elements to the story in order to see their value in the onward progression of the drama. As this is a fairy tale with a literal dark forest and a literal wolf, we will allow ourselves to look a little more deeply at the storyworld and the antagonist in order to get to the heart of this particular version of the story.

Little Red Riding Hood's grandmother doted on her and was always giving her gifts, including the eponymous cloak. The little girl has no other name in the story; she is only known by her attachment to the red cloak made by her grandmother. At the start of the story, Little Red Riding Hood's mother informs her that her grandmother is sick and weak and consequently tasks her daughter with taking her some cake and a bottle of wine, urging her not to leave the path on the way to the grandmother's house, primarily in case she trips and breaks the bottle of wine. Grandmother is clearly very fond of wine.

Little Red Riding Hood, promising to do as her mother tells her, sets out on the half-hour journey through the woods to her grandmother's house. She takes with her the red cloak and the basket of goodies for grandmother. These elements make up her suit of armour in this vanilla take on the story. The cloak makes her recognizable and easy to spot; the basket is a device that she will find useful shortly.

In our storytelling terms, even as she enters the woods, she has not yet entered the story. She is still in her once upon a time, in familiar territory, fulfilling a familiar task; however, almost immediately upon entering the woods, she is approached by the wolf who questions her. Little Red Riding Hood is ridiculously candid and trusting at this point as she lets the wolf know not only that she is heading to Grandma's house to deliver cake and wine but also exactly where Grandma lives: under three large oak trees by the hazel bushes. The wolf immediately sees an opportunity and suggests that Little Red Riding Hood leaves the path and enjoys the flowers and the birds on the long way to Grandma's house. The wolf has other plans.

Here, Little Red Riding Hood accepts the wolf's invitation. Essentially, a deal is struck, and Little Red Riding Hood becomes an unknowing chosen one. She is distracted from the main purpose before her by a third party, the disruptor, and she departs from the path without realizing the ramifications of the arrangement she has just made. As Little Red Riding Hood heads off in search of pretty flowers and the wolf races to Grandma's house, we enter the dark forest of the story.

Now, deep into the drama, the wolf eats the grandmother while Little Red Riding Hood collects flowers. On one side of the wood, the wolf dresses up in Grandma's clothes, tucks himself up in bed and drops off to sleep. On the other side of the wood, Little Red Riding Hood gathers all the flowers that she can gather in her basket before heading to Grandma's house. Here we can see how the path and the experiences off the path create the potential for drama and any tension that exists in this story. Little Red Riding Hood disobeys her mother by travelling off the path but without this transgression there would be no drama to explore. The path represents Little Red Riding Hood's quickest route to the end of the story, but that is not the route that we seek as writers. We seek to pull our chosen ones away from their point of exit because the heart of the story is where the most enjoyable, dramatic and interesting material lies.

The grandmother's house is the gate in this story, but the key to the gate cannot be obtained until the wolf has been vanquished. It is, indeed, the vanquishing of the actual wolf, in this case, that provides the key to the gate. The problem with this story is, of course, that Little Red Riding Hood does not vanquish the wolf. She gets eaten.

As stated earlier, the story of Little Red Riding Hood that we all remember so well from our childhoods is rather unsatisfactory. Little Red Riding Hood doesn't really do anything apart from gather flowers and comment on the size of the wolf's various appendages, and we all know that protagonists should do things. Crucially, the chosen one should be the character that vanquishes the wolf, but, in this case, the real hero arrives in the shape of a random huntsman who happens to be walking past Grandma's house and hears the wolf snoring very loudly. The final act, then, isn't particularly engaging, which is possibly why Perrault left it out. For the completist, though, the huntsman finds the wolf fast asleep, and, worried about harming whatever the wolf has swallowed, he puts down his gun and carefully cuts the wolf open with a pair of scissors. Out jumps Little Red Riding Hood followed by the grandmother. The wolf, surprisingly, remains asleep during which time they pile some stones into his stomach and, when he wakes up and tries to run away, he cannot, so he falls down dead. It feels like the brothers are keen to close the book on this story and get on with the next one; however, we must mention the message first. Little Red Riding Hood promises to never leave the path and run off into the woods again if her mother tells her not to. No wonder there wasn't a Little Red Riding Hood 2. The brothers did actually write a Little Red Riding Hood 2, but it's not really worth the effort.

So, even though this most famous of stories falls short on various aspects of dramatic storytelling, the elements are all there. We find a path; we find drama off the path. There is very definitely a wolf and there is a gate and a key.

Little Red Riding Hood's suit of armour, despite its rather ineffective nature, may be her most famous attribute so it definitely exists as a key element of the story. The story is simple and memorable. The character, unfortunately, is not complex.

On considering this tale, we felt that it would be useful to reinvent the tale in a more dramatically satisfying way following our different pathways. In the next chapter we will take the bare bones of Little Red Riding Hood and retell it as a willing story, an unknowing story, an unable-to-believe story and an accidental story, thereby revealing how each of the elements of the dark forest changes subtly in its nature and use depending on the pathway you decide to utilize. We will also look at the mistaken Little Red Riding Hood, which, in keeping with this most imaginative of pathways, turns out to be quite surprising. In working on the pathways. we will also have to work upon the complexity of our chosen one.

1
The mechanics

Figure 1 *The path, where all great stories begin.*

We have provided you with the basic information about the elements you are going to need in order to navigate a successful screenplay, namely:

- the path
- the gate
- the key
- off the path
- the wolf
- the suit of armour

It is now time to put these elements to work and see how you can use them to build a dramatically effective screenplay. Each of these elements will mean something different or manifest themselves in different ways to your chosen one depending on which pathway they embark upon.

In order to really investigate this phenomenon in some depth, let's reinvent Little Red Riding Hood a number of times, change the pathway and alter the nature and enhance the complexity of the chosen one. If you are using this book as a means to really get the most out of your story and you are already clear on your chosen one's pathway, then by all means cut to the chase and dive into the relevant section, but an overview of the ways in which the elements can be flexible and work as tools for you as a writer might persuade you to read through each of these examples and start to consider what each of these elements means to you and how you can use them to build your narrative into an emotionally engaging, dramatic journey that we all want to embark upon.

So here we go. Let us begin with …

The willing Little Red Riding Hood

The willing chosen one will enter your story with little persuasion. They are heroes who want to right wrongs and overcome wolves, and this doesn't sound very much like Little Red Riding Hood to us. She is a little girl in a handmade cloak making a poor attempt to deliver cakes and wine to Granny while being hoodwinked by a big bad wolf. She's not a natural willing chosen one.

The only contender the fairy tale offers us is the huntsman, the character who actually does something in this story that has a positive impact on the world and allows our characters to exit the dark forest through the gate.

Let's begin with a huntsman, then. Let's imagine he's a lonely man, getting over the death of his pregnant wife who has recently been killed in the forest by a scavenging wolf as she was out picking flowers. The huntsman is hurting, and he's grieving. He's decided to give up his hunting life and live out the rest of his days in lonely isolation mourning the death of his wife and the child they never had together. These are the beginnings of a complex character who is struggling with his own inner demons and has issues to resolve if he is ever going to live a happy life.

He's in town buying provisions one day when the town's mayor accosts him. There's a dangerous lone wolf in the woods, and they need someone to kill it. Many have looked for the wolf, but none have found it. The wolf is wily and intelligent and mean and tricksy. The mayor is calling on the huntsman to come out of retirement and remove this threat from the local area.

The huntsman immediately recognizes all the signs. This was the wolf that killed his wife. He answers the invitation with little hesitation. In keeping with the mindset of the willing chosen one, he determines that he will find this creature and kill it.

Back at his lonely cottage in the woods, the huntsman prepares for the hunt. He sharpens axes and knives. He puts on his stout hiking boots and protective leather jerkin. He studies a map of the dark forest, identifying all of those places where a mean old wolf might hide out.

The course of the story is clear and simple. The huntsman must track, corner and kill the wolf, and the huntsman is well equipped to do this. The act of killing will represent his gate out of the story and, along with it, acceptance for the death of his wife and unborn child, catharsis and an opportunity to return once more to his lonely cottage in the woods and grieve the life he could have lived. His path through the dark forest is prepared. He has identified the wolf's lair. He has prepared himself with what he thinks is his suit of armour. The task in front of him appears simple, and he seems to be well equipped for it. However, the willing chosen one rarely enters the dark forest with the suit of armour required to complete the task in front of them. They find this armour along the way because they do not yet know the true nature of the wolf that awaits them. The unique element that must be a part of the willing narrative is the match; the element in the story that will allow the chosen one to burn the forest. We do not yet know what the match is.

Our huntsman keeps on the path and heads to the wolf's lair only to discover that it is a trap. The wolf is not going to be caught this easily, and the huntsman narrowly escapes a grisly death suddenly finding himself thrust deeper into the dark forest, off the path and having lost his weaponry during the encounter.

Here the huntsman will begin to find that the woods he has known since he was a child is not the place he thought it was. This is a place where innocent victims get lured deeper into the darkest corners by a pack of wolves working with squirrels, badgers, deer, owls and other seemingly innocuous woodland creatures. A network of animals turned into meat-eating fiends by the big bad wolf, the very same wolf who killed the huntsman's wife. No longer is the huntsman seeking a lone wolf with all of his weaponry to hand, but he is looking for the leader of a network of deadly forest dwellers without his weaponry. He also has to shed his protective clothing which allows him to be tracked down by the sensitive noses of the gang of ravening wolves.

Alone in the dark forest now with only his wits for protection and decidedly off the path, the huntsman must devise a plan to defeat the evil at the heart of the forest. At the midpoint of the story, he comes across a frightened group of woodland creatures imprisoned by the gang of wolves. These creatures, unwilling to fall in behind the wolves' diabolical plans, have been put to work for their masters, creating traps in the forest and luring victims into the snares.

The huntsman frees the friendly creatures and together they hatch a plan to defeat the gang by fashioning weapons out of the bones of their victims. Willing chosen ones often gather an army in the dark forest. Here he rebuilds his armour from the tools he finds around him. This is a suit of armour and cache of weapons that will not be detected by the wolf gang, and the last piece of the puzzle falls into place when they come across a wolf lying asleep under a tree, digesting a large meal. Using sharpened bones, the huntsman cuts the wolf open and fashions a suit out of the skin. He is now able to infiltrate the wolf's camp unseen and unsmelt.

This is where he learns the secrets of the gang and hatches the plan to track down and kill the big bad wolf. This plan is the match which will help him to burn the forest, the destiny of all willing chosen ones. When he learns that the big bad wolf has his eyes on a local girl who regularly visits her sick grandmother deep in the woods, the huntsman knows that this information will be the wolf's downfall.

As the rest of the story falls into place and the inevitable end to the big bad wolf closes in, we see the huntsman and his band of woodland creatures band together to trap and kill the wolf. Of course, this will include the 'all is lost' moment so common in films, in which the huntsman arrives too late to save Grandma and Little Red Riding Hood from being eaten but is able, nonetheless, to rescue them from the wolf's stomach, fill it with stones and kill their nemesis.

At the death of the wolves' leader, the woodland creatures all rise up against their enslavers, and the dark forest is burnt to the ground to be replaced by a kinder, fairer and safer wood. The huntsman marries Little Red Riding Hood's mother (why not?), thereby giving him the instant family he so craves.

Thus, the willing Little Red Riding Hood story reveals the elements that make up the heart of the script and the use to which they are put by the prerequisite chosen one. While this reworking of the story is not necessarily a masterpiece of screenwriting skills, it does lay bare the elements of the tale that comprise a willing narrative, and it shows that, in order to work on a simple storyline and give it more emotional and dramatic heart, the first thing you have to do is work on the chosen one and give them more complexity and agency.

For a filmic example that has explicit nods to the tropes within the narrative of Little Red Riding Hood, we could turn to *Hard Candy* (2005), where Hayley traps and tortures Jeff in his house believing that he is a sexual predator who has abused a local girl. Here the marketing clearly points to the source material as an inspiration with a young girl wearing the distinctive red hooded garment from Little Red Riding Hood. Here the ideas within the original story are subverted with Hayley, as the embodiment of Little Red Riding Hood, literally on the hunt for her own form of vigilante justice. Our chosen one stalks the dark forest determined to find a match that will burn it down. During the narrative she learns just how evil the wolf is at the heart of the dark forest and just why he needs to be destroyed.

The unknowing Little Red Riding Hood

As we have already ascertained, Little Red Riding Hood is already, in essence, an unknowing story. But we have also ascertained that Little Red Riding Hood is the wrong protagonist as she doesn't actually take any action in the story to overcome the forces ranged against her. In order to retell the story using her as a genuine unknowing chosen one, we are going to have to make some changes.

If we keep the existing story as is and rejoin it at the invitation, then we can start to build a mid-section that gives us an opportunity to explore character, motivation and drama in much more depth and build the complexity in the chosen one that is so lacking in the original tale.

So, Little Red Riding Hood, who is quite happily living her best life delivering much needed sustenance to her ageing granny, does a deal with a seemingly innocuous wolf she meets in the woods. This is the key moment for chosen ones on this pathway. They are diverted from their planned route through life by a disruptor. The disruptor is occasionally but not normally the big bad wolf, and the disruptor will normally ask them to fulfil a task with a finite conclusion that appears to be easily realizable for the unknowing chosen one. For this moment to work more effectively, and to give us material to explore in the heart of the screenplay, we're going to have to add an extra element here.

Given that the huntsman is not bedded into the existing fairy story, now might be a good time to introduce him via a storyline that would bring him more into the body of the narrative. How about if Little Red Riding Hood, on her way to Grandma's house, and on the path, spots something in the bushes a little way off the path? This sounds much more interesting.

Little Red Riding Hood goes to investigate and finds a man, badly mauled and bleeding out: a huntsman who has been attacked by a wolf and is clinging on to life by a thread. The huntsman begs her to help him to his cottage. It's not far, and he can recuperate there. Who would turn down such a straightforward deal? Little Red Riding Hood naturally agrees to help. She's always agreeing to requests from total strangers.

They make it to the huntsman's cottage most definitively even further off the path, but there is a clear sense that they are being watched and followed. Arriving at the small wooden hut, the huntsman orders Little Red Riding Hood to lock all the doors and shutter all the windows. He clearly hasn't told her the whole story about his feud with the wolf, but now it comes out. The wolf only spared his life on the proviso that he would bring him a child to devour – a much tastier and more tender meal for a hungry wolf.

The huntsman laid it on a bit thick with his life-threatening injuries in order to lure Little Red Riding Hood to the cottage, but now he's beginning to regret the deal. She is so sweet and trusting. Here we reach the unique element of the unknowing storyline in the appearance of the first gate. There are two gates in this narrative, and the first is reached fairly easily. The chosen one treads a direct path from the invitation to the first gate imagining that this will free them from the deal and from the story, but the first gate is a trick played upon the chosen one by the disruptor. The first gate opens to reveal a much larger dark forest beyond, and the only way to reach the second gate is off the path.

Little Red Riding Hood wears a home-made red cloak, which is extremely noticeable and identifies her as an innocent child. This is her suit of armour as she enters the dark forest, but, typically, the unknowing chosen one must shed their suit of armour as they realize the lie behind the deal they have struck and realize that their suit of armour does them no favours. She can no longer be the innocent, trusting little girl if she wants to get out of this story in one piece. She needs to shed the trappings of innocence and embrace her destiny if she wants to find the key to the second gate and defeat the wolf.

The nature of the key on the unknowing pathway is discovered when the truth of the uneven bargain reveals itself. The key to unlocking the gate in this story often requires the chosen one to jettison a moment in their past which has been holding them back or that they have been holding on to too closely for too long.

Little Red Riding Hood admits to the huntsman, as they cower in his cottage deep, deep in the dark forest and the wolf prowls outside just waiting for his opportunity to attack, that her grandmother died a year ago. These trips into the woods to deliver cake and wine have only been to hide the truth from her mother. The sweet, naive Little Red Riding Hood of the story has just become more complex … and interesting. Grandma's house, without Grandma, has become a haven for her. Her own place deep in the woods where she can enjoy cake and wine and practise the sport that her mother hates so much: karate.

Now that the truth is out for both of them, the course is set for the defeat of the wolf based on honesty, openness and mutual understanding. The unknowing story arc is full of half-truths, secrets and lies. Only when these elements are laid bare and rejected can the key to the gate be found. In fact, the truth is the key to the gate. Only through total openness can the terms and conditions of the unfair bargain be reversed and the deal undone.

The denouement of this story will see the huntsman and Little Red Riding Hood defeat the wolf through their combined skills and through Riding Hood jettisoning her adopted persona of the young, innocent child and adopting the kick-ass persona of the karate master. She will no longer be Little Red Riding Hood as she exits the gate, she will be larger, and probably not wearing a hood, but if she is, definitely not a red one.

An unknowing Little Red Riding Hood on the big screen could be Andy from *The Devil Wears Prada* (2006). Here, Little Red Riding Hood is an aspiring journalist who has no other option but to take the job offered to her. She steps unwillingly and nervously into *Runway* magazine, a frightening and dense dark forest, and faces up to editor-in-chief, Miranda Priestly, a terrifying wolf. During the narrative, Andy realizes, like all good unknowing chosen ones, that the dark forest she first entered into is not at all what she thought it was, and this will require her to find a way out of the deal that she has made to escape it unharmed. All of the mechanics and ideas are there, it is just that they are now wrapped in the world of high fashion.

The unable-to-believe Little Red Riding Hood

There are a couple of key elements we need to include when conjuring up an unable-to-believe storyline. First, the chosen one must be hampered by the impression that they are unworthy of succeeding in their story world, and, second, they need to have a clear goal that, to them, is unattainable. Most importantly, the unable-to-believe chosen one will also need a mentor or tormentor to give them that belief they are so lacking. This is the element which is unique to this storyline and essential to all unable-to-believe storylines. This means we're going to have to make some more changes to Little Red Riding Hood.

Let's begin in the village school with a little boy of ten or eleven years who's good at maths. Unfortunately, the world of woods, wolves and grandmas doesn't value maths whizzery, and this poor kid also happens to be the son of the most revered huntsman in the vicinity. The huntsman is ashamed of his son's inability to hunt, snare, kill or skin anything, and the son is embarrassed and bullied by the other local kids.

There is only one in the school who shows any kindness towards our hapless chosen one, and this is a little girl with a distinctive red cloak. Our nerdy maths kid falls for this thoughtful, generous, sweet girl. There is scope for some nice, complex character work here as two quirky, oddball children play off against one another. Taika Waititi loves playing with these kinds of characters.

As the nerdy huntsman's son grows towards manhood and his hunting skills do not improve, a terrible event happens when his father is killed by a wolf while out on a hunt. It is the accepted lore of the land that the son should avenge the untimely death of the father, and our hapless chosen one feels entirely ill equipped for the task in front of him. He decides the best thing he can do is simply leave town. Little Red Riding Hood begs him to stay and tells him that her grandfather will help him. Our hero simply laughs. Her grandfather is the town drunk who spends his days either knocking back beers at the local bar or lying in a gutter sleeping them off.

But our chosen one really doesn't want to leave Little Red Riding Hood and the future he sees for them both, so he decides to meet with the old man … who will become his mentor.

At this point, the huntsman's son accepts the invitation. This is the most unwilling of all chosen ones, and they really do not want to be in this story at all. The narrative in front of them will see them straying again and again from the path, and it will be the mentor who will pull them back on, pointing to the gate so clearly visible at the end of the path.

The relationship between the grandfather and the young man will be a rocky one, but the grandfather will see something in the young man that he himself doesn't see. Unlike other journeys through the dark forest, it is off the path where this chosen one feels most safe and secure. Our chosen one would rather be reading beneath a tree out of sight of others than practising for the hunt with axes and knives. But the grandfather offers a different type of mentorship which, crucially, our young man doesn't understand or fully believe in. The grandfather urges the chosen one to further embrace his strengths. They discuss maths in all its forms: probability, mechanics, geometry, trigonometry and statistics. The young man is angered by this waste of time and energy. How will maths ever help him to avenge the death of his father?

The unable-to-believe chosen one enters the dark forest with a suit of armour that they do not believe has any worth. It is dented, rusted over, cumbersome and ugly, but this is the same suit of armour that will see them discover the key that will enable them to open the gate.

The grandfather's habitual state of inebriation means that Little Red Riding Hood has to regularly deliver cake and wine to her beloved grandmother on the other side of the woods. This despite the fact that her grandfather is rarely home. On this particular, fateful day our hero is revising calculus at the back of the bar while Grandfather works his way through a bottle of whisky when news comes through that the wolf has been spotted in the woods. The village expects our chosen one to step up and do away with the creature once and for all, but he definitely doesn't feel ready. However, when the news of the wolf's reappearance is married with further information that Little Red Riding Hood is out on one of her Grandma deliveries through his hunting grounds, he must do something.

He begins to equip himself with all the necessary weaponry to defeat the wolf, but the half-cut grandfather tells him he doesn't need any of that. He'll know what he needs when the time comes. Full of self-doubt, our chosen one heads into the woods and straight to Grandma's house where the final battle must take place. Little Red Riding Hood is just telling Grandma how large her eyes are and how sharp her teeth are when our hero casts around him. What can he do to stop the inevitable?

The answer, of course, is maths. In a big set piece, our chosen one is able to defeat the wolf through embracing his inherent skills. Angles, trajectories, weight and velocity are all powerful tools when used as weaponry, and the wolf doesn't stand a chance. The unable-to-believe chosen one has found the key deep within themselves. They had it all along, but they had to believe in themselves in order to access it, and their mentor gave them that belief. Their suit of armour is the same as that which they entered the dark forest wearing. The gate was always going to be right where it is: deep in the woods with the death of the wolf. The unable-to-believe chosen one must overcome their own self-doubt in order to become a swan.

For a filmic example of a story, we can look to *The Matrix* (1999) where chosen one Neo (his very name an anagram of '[the] One') comes to learn that he lives in a future that is merely a simulation created to distract humans as a race of robots turn their physical bodies into batteries. When Neo's mentor Morpheus offers him a choice of the red pill or the blue pill during the invitation stage of the narrative, Neo is setting himself off on a path towards uncovering the swan inside him and becoming the hero who will eventually lead humanity out of its slumber and servitude. The dark forest for Neo is one that literally takes place in his mind as he realizes the abilities that he has within himself to master the simulation that humanity is trapped inside. There are several moments where Neo veers off the path to question if he is 'The One' that Morpheus believes he is; however, the unwavering support that he has from his mentor figure is proved correct during the last throw of the dice where he is able to put all of the lessons Morpheus has been teaching him into practice and finally defeat Agent Smith, the wolf who has stalked the dark forest from the beginning. Our character of Little Red Riding Hood can be taken across genres, locations, tones and styles, but the mechanics of her story can clearly be seen on screen.

The accidental Little Red Riding Hood

Accidental storylines can be enormous fun to invent. They will often, but not always, involve a magical element by which aegis our chosen one finds themselves in an unfamiliar world, unsure of how to get home. The whole story is working its way towards the return, when the chosen one is able to find the key that enables them to open the gate and return to their once upon a time. The secret to writing a successful accidental narrative is in marrying geography and psychology in a dramatically satisfying way. The strange world that the chosen one inhabits must somehow reflect their own conflicted nature. The obvious chosen one to select for an accidental telling of this fairy story is Little Red Riding Hood herself, but we're going to have to play with her character a little.

Present-day Little Red Riding Hood is a student of ethnography at a prestigious university in the heart of Bavaria, studying fairy stories and folk tales and sourcing original texts at the library. She is an amazing linguist, able to decipher texts that previous readers may have glossed over. But she is also deeply unpopular with her peers and the wider faculty. She is rude and full of her own self-importance – a complex and conflicted character.

Through her research work, she comes across an ancient telling of the Little Red Riding Hood story, predating Perrault and Grimm by a thousand years. The source tells the story as if it were based on truth and even gives an exact location deep in a forest close to the Czech border. Little Red Riding Hood applies for, and receives, a research grant and heads to the forest to find out more, trekking into the heart of the ancient woodland, a lonely and mysterious place.

Losing her way and feeling very cold, she finds a cloak beneath a tree in which she wraps herself. A red cloak. Hungry and tired, she comes across an ancient cottage, miles from anywhere, knocks and enters at the sound of a gruff voice. Making her way to the bedroom, she finds a weird old lady in bed wrapped in blankets and wearing a low bonnet. Our chosen one can't help but notice that the old lady has very big eyes … a very big nose … very big teeth …

She barely makes it out of there before the wolf leaps from the bed, all the better to eat her. Slamming the door closed, she escapes into the surrounding woodland, which has subtly changed. No longer is she in a Bavarian forest in the twenty-first century: she has been transported to the fairy-tale world of Little Red Riding Hood, confirmed to her by the Three Little Pigs shouting 'hello' to her as they pass, seven dwarves heading off to work with pickaxes and a young man trying to plant a beanstalk on a patch of fertile ground.

This pathway is all about trying to find the way home and, for our chosen one deep in the land of fairy tales, the gate appears obvious. The end of the story of Little Red Riding Hood involves a huntsman killing the wolf. Find the huntsman, kill the wolf, and, Bob's your uncle, she can go home and write up her dissertation. We know it's never going to be that simple. Yes, our heroine can seek out the local huntsman and organize a way to trap and kill the wolf, but she clearly has a lesson to learn here. The gate is generally clearly visible to the accidental chosen one. They know how they should be able to return to their once upon a time, but it doesn't work. The world that they have been transported to needs to work their magic on them, and they need to grow as individuals before they are set free. Therefore, there is going to be a unique element in the accidental narrative, and that unique element is going to be the gatekeeper – in this case, the huntsman.

So, our chosen one meets up with the huntsman and demands release from the story world in her usual overbearing and self-entitled manner. The huntsman tells our chosen one that, yes, he can kill the wolf, but he won't. Not until she's done something for him. The role of the gatekeeper is to prevent the accidental chosen one from passing through the gate until they have learned the lesson that must be learned in the accidental story world.

Once again, the real story is off the path. Our rude researcher must do the bidding of the huntsman so that she will be able to find the key and return home. The dark forest is really the wolf on this pathway. It is alien, dangerous and threatens to keep our chosen one here forever. Many accidental storylines do not have a literal wolf, but we do, of course.

The suit of armour manifests itself differently here to other story pathways. To all intents and purposes, the chosen one has no suit of armour. They are entirely at sea in an alien landscape, unsure of how to navigate this space, but this is a storyline all about coming to understand one's own conflicted nature, and our chosen one will realize that they had both the suit of armour and the key with them the whole time. They just had to dig deep to recognize that fact.

Our particular chosen one is possessed with knowledge which will help her to negotiate the dark forest and to make friends (and enemies), but she will have to learn that she is not as special as she thinks she is if she is ever going to leave this place. She will learn to respect others and discover that real life can be more exciting and meaningful than the words found in a dusty old academic book. As with all of these stories, it is the complexity of her character that will render this simple tale engaging and sustain the story through the 100 pages we need to write if we're ever going to sell this to a major Hollywood studio.

For our accidental Little Red Riding Hood, we might look to Haley in *Crawl* (2019). Here our young chosen one is an adept college swimmer who is sucked into a dark forest that takes place entirely in the crawl space of her father's house during a hurricane. Haley must navigate this terrifying space to try and get her injured father out of danger as the water rises around her. All the while, she is hindered by a wolf that, in this instance, is a large alligator – a wolf that is literally trying to eat her as she ventures towards the gate she is desperate to reach. It is now our Little Red Riding Hood's job to escape the terrifying dark forest that she has ended up in while keeping her father safe from harm.

The mistaken Little Red Riding Hood

The mistaken pathway is where the anti-hero resides. Each pathway outlined above has their own negative reflection. Chosen ones who lose their path and never rediscover them, chosen ones who search in vain for mentors, chosen ones who never become swans …

Mistaken story arcs are much less prescriptive in their make-up than their 'positive' cousins, but it is certainly possible to point to ideas for storylines inhabiting this realm and see that each of the elements we have displayed in the preceding narratives remains as valuable and useful to you, the writer of these potentially disturbing storylines.

The mistaken/willing chosen one is a protagonist who will accept the invitation immediately and participate thoroughly in the storyline, but their character will move them in a different direction. The gate will become less important to them as they become more enamoured with the dark forest. In our proposed willing storyline, the mistaken version will see our chosen one seeing the possibilities behind the wolf's network of woodland creatures. He will kill the wolf and take over the operation. The gate disappears. Off the path becomes his home. His suit of armour protects him from the people who hired him rather than the creatures that he enslaves. He throws the key away. He loves it here.

The mistaken/unknowing chosen one has no honesty, openness or mutual understanding. As Little Red Riding Hood and the huntsman hide in the cottage preparing for the attack of the wolf, Little Red Riding Hood sees that she signed an unfair deal but has no intention of undoing it. She is an anti-hero, so she will use the vulnerable huntsman to do a deal with the wolf to attempt to escape her predicament. But nobody in the world of mistaken storylines is trustworthy, and this action will lead to a confrontation with the wolf which she will either win or lose depending on the nature of the screenplay. Once again, there is no gate. There is no escaping this story because of the actions of the chosen one. Little Red Riding Hood will have to reap the rewards of her mistaken deal.

The mistaken/unable-to-believe chosen one is searching for a mentor that they will never find. The young maths whizz never discovers the true worth of his skills and so fails to defeat the wolf. It is a truth of all mistaken storylines that they will never leave the dark forest except through death, and, therefore, we have a choice with this tale: that it should either become the story of a chosen one who sides with the wolf in order to survive and thrive in the dark forest or this is a slasher movie in which our hapless, helpless, mentorless chosen one is stalked by the wolf and never manages to achieve any of the greatness which is buried within.

The mistaken/accidental storyline is almost always a horror. The strange land into which our chosen one is thrust has no way out, and there will never be a return to the once-upon-a-time. The wolf is the serial killer or the monster or the ghost or the alien from so many familiar horrors, and our chosen one is the final girl, destined to pit herself against the darkness in the face of certain death. Our pompous university researcher may well realize the error of her ways, but this realization will come too late for her. If she doesn't die in this dark forest, she will definitely die in the sequel.

As mentioned previously, the mistaken paradigm is a subversion of the ideas of the other four pathways and therefore has a variety of examples that could be given within the canon of work. However, it is also the paradigm that it could be argued that the original story of Little Red Riding Hood leans the closest towards both tonally and thematically. With its inherently horrific ideas and the broader implications of it being a coming-of-age narrative, the piece could be a model for some of the most memorable horror narratives from cinema.

The Wicker Man (1973) sees Sergeant Neil Howie sent to the island of Summerisle to investigate the disappearance of a young girl. Howie is revolted to learn that the inhabitants of the island worship pagan gods and have great plans for the officer during their May Day celebrations. He begins to become lost within the dark forest of Summerisle and eventually is trapped within the 'belly' of a large wicker man statue where he is burnt to death by the community on the island as a sacrifice in the hope of them appeasing their gods and receiving a favourable harvest.

As you can see, the story may change, the chosen one may change, and the motivation may change, but the core elements to the story remain important regardless of the tale being told, and the presence of an extra element in each of the pathways provides an additional tool for you, as the writer, developing these stories. These elements will be incredibly useful to you as you develop your stories through the central acts of the screenplay. We will explore how they work in more depth as you read further, but now you can see how they create clear signposts, moments of change and obstacles for our chosen ones as they move through the story.

As we have already expressed, at the heart of your simple story is a complex character, and, as we consider the key elements that make up the heart of the script, let us also consider the emotional and psychological journey that your chosen one must take if we are to engage with them on their adventures.

'Who am I?'

At the opening of your story, imagine your chosen one asking the question, 'Who Am I?' Then think of what the answer to this question is, for them. Then imagine them asking themselves the same question at the end of the story. Is the answer different?

Andrew Stanton puts this brilliantly in his TED Talk on the subject of storytelling when he explores the last-throw-of-the-dice moment in *Lawrence of Arabia* (1962). Having journeyed across the Sinai desert, a lone motorcyclist calls out to Lawrence, 'Who are you?' An innocent question within the diegesis of the narrative. There is a war on, and the man has to verify who these soldiers emerging from the sands are. However, dramaturgically, it challenges Lawrence and has him question if the man who started this journey is the same one who has finished it.

The same is true for Sarya in *My Small Land* (2022). As a Kurdish refugee in Japan, she is desperate to be able to assimilate into the notoriously closed-off culture. With her father desperate for her to remain true to her roots, he continues to remind her that their future is not on the island nation. Torn between two cultures, in the end she finds balance between the two identities within her as she plays with her younger brother in a makeshift world that embraces all facets of who they are. Sally in *The Texas Chainsaw Massacre* (1974) comes to believe that she is a victim as she is captured by the cannibalistic family of the narrative. However, come the end, she responds to this question by asserting that she is in fact a survivor and the first of many final girls who will tread similar paths.

However, within the pathways of our respective chosen ones, we can mine this question further. Rather than asking themselves, 'Who am I?'

at the beginning and end of your screenplay, have them ask themselves the same question at the moment of invitation, at the midpoint, at the 'all is lost' moment. Are the answers different? If not, why not? Is your complex character changing? If not, why not? Maybe they are not complex enough. Within each paradigm, we can also have the question alter slightly to ensure that your chosen one is constantly active in the pursuit of an answer that will assist in driving both the simple plot and the complex character(s) within the piece. These will be explored in detail in the respective chapters for each paradigm. However, they all point back to the notion that your chosen one is looking to understand that all important question that should be at the root of all good drama: 'Who am I?'

Always ensure that you have this question in the back of your mind when constructing the scenes and sequences within the heart of your screenplay so that your writing and your character are continually developing in line with the central question of the piece.

Now that we have given a general overview of the story elements and seen them at play in a familiar tale, it's time to go much more in depth and explore how these elements manifest themselves on film, still remembering the core lesson of this book as we move forward: *Simple story, complex characters.*

2

Willing

Figure 2 *Your willing chosen one must find a key to unlock their story.*

As you embark on your adventure alongside the willing chosen one, bear in mind that these are narratives of white knights hacking through dense undergrowth to slay dragons, rescue princesses and save villages. Some writers give narratives like this a wide berth believing them to be formulaic popcorn fodder; however, what can be seen as a weakness is also the paradigm's greatest strength. If you decide to travel down this story pathway, you will be able to deliver to an audience exactly the cinema-going experience they crave. With their desires fulfilled, you will be known as the writer who justified the expense of the multiplex, the train into town and the babysitter waiting at home – an honour that those who wade in the murky world of the 'art house' will never be able to place upon their mantle.

The greatest roadmap for the willing arc in film comes from Akira Kurosawa's *Seven Samurai* (1954) in which a veteran swordsmith heads to find six other samurai who will assist in protecting a village from marauding bandits. Not only is it a brilliant piece of work, but it has been an influence on many successful films since its release, from John Sturges's Western remake, *The Magnificent Seven* (1961), to the lowly ants rescuing the village from the ravening locusts in *A Bug's Life* (1999), right up to the poor farmers of Veldt against the sadistic Imperium in *Rebel Moon* (2023). In each of these examples, the chosen ones follow closely in the footsteps of those seven samurai. Kurosawa's characters have been called on to protect every corner of the known universe from faraway stars to anthills at our feet. It is an arc that so perfectly encompasses the themes, tone and structure of the willing paradigm that any screenwriter wishing to write such a piece has to be intimately familiar with how it works. Most importantly though, the piece acknowledges one of the more important mechanics within the paradigm: that of gathering a team around the chosen one, which allows them to grow and to see the weaknesses within the armour that they were blind to at the beginning, thereby paving the way for them to become the true chosen one they were always destined to be.

What is at the heart of the willing narrative?

The willing paradigm pits the greatest of enemies against one another. Light fights dark. Good triumphs over evil. Truth defeats lies. Freedom slays tyranny. At the heart of every willing arc, there must be this fundamental idea that runs the whole of the narrative and informs all of the choices that our chosen one makes during it.

The value of these narratives is that an audience can experience the pinnacle of human conflict(s) without the fear of having to actually go through them themselves. They will see a fight for justice play out across the screen during the runtime, whatever that means in this version of the story that you are telling. As you pen the willing narrative, the verb 'to fight' is an important one. It not only alludes to the complex personality of the chosen one who is willing to do what needs to be done in order to save the day, but also gives them an agency that is beyond that of their peers who are travelling the other narrative pathways. Furthermore, the verb 'to fight' already suggests the equal yet opposite force that comes from the wolves of these stories. They, just like our chosen ones, will not go down without a fight – a fight that, within the parameters of the tone you have established, will be big and bloody.

The dark forest you create for the willing chosen one must be one where these two forces initially coexist in some capacity with the more malevolent of the two initially dominant, but, following the arrival of our chosen one, their days will be numbered. However, this reversal of dominance will not happen swiftly or easily. Our chosen one may be adept, but they have never been on an adventure like this or have even been challenged in the way that this particular dark forest will challenge them.

In the moment of the invitation, your chosen one asks themselves the question, 'Who am I?' They are the bravest of their community so answer willingly that they are the individual who is capable of righting the wrong, defending the defenceless and dealing with the immediate danger they are faced with. However, as they venture through the dark forest, they will realize that the task that they initially thought would only save those closest to them has become the task of saving the world as they know it. The answer to that fundamental question will change as they discover that the terrorist who kidnapped the Archbishop of Canterbury actually has a cache of nuclear bombs, and they are planning to blow up every church in the city; or that the giant octopus that has been tearing ships apart in the Atlantic Ocean is actually a super-intelligent creature from the Lost City of Atlantis; or that the mean teacher who has been confiscating the kids' phones is actually a tech whizz who has been dismantling them and building an evil supercomputer. It's the 'We're going to need a bigger boat' moment that occurs in every willing narrative.

For our willing chosen ones, they are always looking to solve the problems that are presented to them straight away. However, the scope and scale of the problem merely expand as the narrative continues. They must go on a journey to understand the evil at the heart of the dark forest and how it is that they are going to destroy it. The question that fulfils their 'Who am I?' becomes 'What can I do to fix this?' Joy from *Inside Out 2* (2024) is constantly asking herself this very question as she and the other emotions journey through the dark forest of Riley's mind. With Anxiety at the controls up in Headquarters, the task goes from preventing short-term damage to Riley's relationships in the real world to the very real danger of Anxiety taking over her sense of self. Pushing your chosen one to have to fight to find the answer to this question ensures that they are forever active in pushing forward to a solution to the central dramatic question of the piece that you have proposed.

Finally, it is important to note here that this ramping up of the stakes does not make the story more complex: it makes the same story more challenging.

For example, in *Jaws* (1975), the shark does not change the challenge before Quint, Hooper and Brody: it changes the scale of the challenge.

The key: Strike the match

Ultimately, the path for our chosen one ends with them in a place where they must burn the forest. During their journey through the dark forest, they have come to learn of the evil(s) that lurk there and must find a way to light the fire to do this. We call this element the match. This is the unique element of the willing arc that helps them when they alter their trajectory from their relatively small goal to saving the world as they know it. The only way to do this is to render the dark forest they have journeyed through to ash. The key is ultimately the thing that allows them to find the answer to their question, 'What can I do to fix this?'

The match is often something that the chosen one must find deep within the darkest corners of the dark forest. This object of desire is something that both chosen one and the wolf are searching for. In more traditional parlance, this might be seen as a Hitchcockian MacGuffin – a transparent but effective writing tool that can assist a writer in developing a clear path for the chosen one.

However, as a dramaturgical technique, the MacGuffin has evolved over time. This isn't to say that the willing paradigm isn't the only one where a MacGuffin can be used to aid with the narrative momentum, but the use of the match in being a tool to burn the forest is particular to the willing narrative and therefore this is often where we see the MacGuffin used in the most effective ways to propel a narrative forward.

There are some strategies that you can use to effectively develop this element of your writing. First, you could cloak your object of desire in a mystery. In *Men in Black* (1997), Agents J and K are tasked with saving the world from an alien invasion and spend large portions of the film searching for Orion's Belt after receiving a cryptic clue from an alien visitor. However, it isn't until much later in the film that we learn the true nature of this artefact. By the time the pair have discovered this, there are much greater conflicts in which our chosen one (and the rest of the planet) are involved.

You could raise the stakes by considering why your character is after the object as they move through the acts. *Indiana Jones and The Last Crusade* (1989), in which our chosen one seeks out the Holy Grail with his father in tow, does this brilliantly. Having reached the site of the Grail, Indy is forced to go and retrieve it from the cavern in order to save his father who has just been shot. The stakes were high enough as our intrepid adventurers raced against the Nazis to snatch the artefact, but with the introduction of personal stakes for Indy, we are further invested in his mission to retrieve it.

A different approach to this would be to make the match dangerous to hold on to in the first place. In *The Lord of the Rings: The Return of the King* (2003), we see that Frodo is slowly succumbing to the ring's temptations, and the longer he has it in his possession, the more likely it is that he will eventually wither away to become a creature like Gollum. Another example is the diamond sought by Harley Quinn in *Birds of Prey (and the Fantabulous Emancipation of One Harley Quinn)* (2020). Although there is plenty of exposition about account numbers and vast fortunes that are supposed to make us care about this artefact, we are only truly invested in the mission once Cassandra Cain has swallowed the diamond in an attempt to hide it, not realizing that Roman Sionis isn't above slicing her open to get it out. It now becomes a race against time to retrieve the diamond from her while keeping her safe. These objects of desire work so well because there are ticking clocks associated with them. The journey to see their destiny fulfilled as the match used to burn the forest has to be completed before the time runs out, and therefore drama and urgency is automatically created around them.

Another option would be to give your match some humanity. An audience is less inclined to emotionally connect to things than they are to connect to people. If the match you are creating has some humanlike qualities, the audience is far more likely to feel empathetic towards it and therefore invest in its fate. Both *Saving Private Ryan* (1998) and *The Hangover* (2009) have our heroes looking for Ryan and Doug, respectively, characters we do not meet until the penultimate act of the films. It is the search for them that is the driving force for the external journeys our characters are on.

Finally, you might decide on a meta approach to your match in the knowledge that, even the casual cinemagoer will be familiar with the construction of your narrative around the object of desire. It is a trope firmly cemented in the pop-culture landscape, after all. Rather than draw the derision of your audience, you could give your object such a contrived name that the audience understands that they too are in on the joke which is that this is something which could only exist within the landscape of the movie. Both *Avatar*'s (2009) Unobtainium and *The Lego Movie*'s (2014) 'Piece of Resistance' are a nod and a wink to the audience. Both of these allow for the work to effectively establish the tone within this element of the narrative.

In some cases, your chosen one may discover their match much earlier in the dark forest, but it isn't until much later in their journey that they understand its importance. A clear example of this is in *The Hunger Games* (2012) where Katniss finds the berries which she will leverage at the end to force the powers in Panem to declare two winners of the competition of which she and Peeta are part. Although the dark forest isn't fully burnt as the first instalment of the franchise comes to a close, it is certainly singed, and the fires of revolution are starting to be lit across the dystopian nation.

Finally, the chosen ones may have brought the match into the dark forest with them as they transitioned between Acts 1 and 2, but they have only just realized its worth. In investment banking satire *Dumb Money* (2023), Keith's status as an underdog, his oddball demeanour and the support that he has of his family are the things that will burn the dark forest as he is able to harness all of these elements to showcase during the remote Congressional hearing and prove that what he (and countless others) are doing is not only legal but actually exactly what the stock market is supposed to be for.

It is Koichi's desire to live and make something of his life in *Godzilla Minus One* (2023) that allows him to finally defeat Godzilla in the closing minutes of the film. When we first meet him, he was supposed to have completed a kamikaze mission in the dying days of the Second World War; however, he lands on a remote island in the Sea of Japan claiming that he had troubles with his plane that prevented him from going through with the act. Now, armed with an ejector seat fashioned by a mechanic, he can destroy Godzilla and live to fight another day. He metaphorically defeats the long shadow of the war that looms over the film while showcasing his special skill of being a pilot for which he has trained for during the narrative.

The match is one of the most useful tools you will discover as you build your willing narrative. Consider the nature of the dark forest and the wolf in deciding what you would like your match to be. What object, artefact, character or hidden talent do you need to set up in your storyline to bring to bear on the dark forest at the exact moment that your chosen one will need it the most? What is it that your chosen one could eventually find within the dark forest that will allow them to destroy the evil that resides at the heart of your dark forest?

The path: Well-trodden but uphill

As previously mentioned, the dark forest of your story is a space which the chosen one knows and possibly knows well. Keith Gill (*Roaring Kitty*) understands the financial world incredibly well in *Dumb Money*; Koichi Shikishima has already come face to face with Godzilla in the prologue of *Godzilla Minus One*; and Sarah, in *Help* (2021), is well established as a caregiver in the assisted-living facility where she works. They have been expecting that one day an invitation such as the one they are about to receive might come their way and are able to grasp it with both hands when it does arrive. However, as they journey through this space, they will begin to understand that no matter how adept they are, this will be an experience that will take all of their skills to overcome. Their familiarity with the dark forest will only take them so far. At all times though, it is clear that this challenge is their burden to carry. They are, after all, the chosen one who has been selected for this task.

You will find it useful, as you plan your storyline, to give us a clear indication how close or far away our chosen one is from achieving their goal. There can be a mystery that needs to be solved along the way, and therefore there may be a clue that you must hide from the audience and our chosen one; however, the path that they are on must point towards the gate where the final confrontation with the wolf ends. Keith in *Dumb Money* will finally have to answer to the hedge funds that he is in the process of humiliating; Koichi is destined to have to face off with Godzilla in *Godzilla Minus One*; and Sarah will end up challenging the very establishment that further exacerbated the dilemmas she faced within her own terrifying dark forest.

The narrative of a willing arc is one that must feel as if it is forever being pushed forward by the chosen one. They are active agents of change who deliberately and purposefully affect everything around them. They must constantly be making choices that they have instigated. Frequently headstrong and single-minded, they will have to learn how to play nice and share at some point, but they have to be able to move the narrative along through the sheer force of their will. Ethan Hunt, John Wick and Katniss Everdeen are not ones to sit back and allow things to happen to them.

As they continue their journey on the path, the willing chosen one faces increasingly more difficult odds. The conflict they initially thought they could deal with on their own has grown larger and more dangerous than they could have imagined, and they are forced to take on allies, now endangering others who they feel an acute responsibility for. As they journey toward the last throw of the dice, our chosen one will leave their allies silently in the night before the conflict ensuring that no one can follow them, or they will insist that they must complete this last challenge alone. Often though, they do not fully understand that they have inspired the team they have assembled, and the allies, too, are willing to risk their lives for a cause that they believe in. Their allies will of course follow them and intervene at the most crucial and dramatically satisfactory moment. Keith in *Dumb Money* must face the Congressional hearing alone in his basement, lamenting that he has potentially harmed his growing family in his crusade against Wall Street. However, his wife sits at the foot of the stairs ensuring that he is able to find the courage to say the things that he needs to say to those quizzing him. Thus far, in their single-mindedness, they have only ever journeyed on the path and have yet to explore the deepest and darkest parts of the forest where the internal adventure lies for them.

Off the path: Telling scary stories by the campfire

This is the space within the dark forest where two distinct things happen for our chosen one: first, it is where your chosen one gathers and then bonds with their allies who will be a core part of the narrative in developing the surrogate family that our chosen one builds around them; second, your chosen one will gain an understanding that this dark forest holds even darker secrets than they first imagined within its shadows, and the only way to prevent the harm that is there is to burn it to the ground.

As your chosen one ventures off the path, there is a marked change in tone and pacing of the narrative. You as the writer are able to slow everything down and give your chosen one a moment or two alone with the allies they are in the process of getting to know. During the beginnings of their exploration of the dark forest, your chosen one will still attempt to assert the special status that they held within their Act 1. They will deliberately remove themselves, either physically or emotionally, from those who they feel offer nothing to the journey they are on. They will purposefully close themselves off and withhold elements of their personality from those around them. Whatever it is that they are withholding is a gift for a writer here as it allows for this information to be slowly teased out as the narrative progresses. You will be able to unwrap their hidden facets through these 'campfire moments' where they begin to transition through their emotional and psychological transformation. They will spill secrets and divulge stories of their past that plague them as the answer to the question 'What can I do to fix this?' gradually changes. All of these things will build trust between the allies and allow them to outline their conflicted nature to the team.

These moments also allow us to see that our chosen one isn't the machine-like agent of change as they begin to admit or at least acknowledge their failings. Furthermore, they will begin to recognize the skills that they lack from their physical repertoire – the skills for which their allies will be the perfect complement. Often these shortcomings will be directly linked to their conflicted nature. In *Dumb Money*, Keith discusses his faltering belief in his scheme only to be told by his wife that he should continue as the movement that he has started around his Gamestop stock purchases needs him. In one of the more harrowing scenes in *Help*, Sarah must wake Tony, a resident who lives in the facility where she works, to assist her in moving another resident who has COVID-19 onto his front so that he can breathe. Her choice here is one of desperation and staying true to her character and pathway. She does everything in her power to ensure that Tony, once brought onto the path, is kept as safe as possible.

The power of a filmic narrative also allows us in the audience to have a privileged position where we can see our wolf at work off the path. Here they act out their malevolent schemes in full view of us so that we can not just gain an understanding of their twisted ideology but also realize for ourselves why this dark forest needs to be burnt. Typically, these elements are accompanied by something of a moustache-twirling monologue from the wolf that outlines how they see the dark forest they built, the contrary ideological outlook they have to the chosen one and the hatred that they have for them and the fact that they have derailed their best-laid plans.

Atticus Noble laments Kora's current trajectory in *Rebel Moon* that will bring them face to face. In *A Bug's Life*, Hopper delivers a monologue not just about how the grasshoppers will crush the ant colony further no matter if they reach their targets or not but also the broader evils of unchecked modern capitalist production (not bad for a children's film). In *Dumb Money*, we frequently cut to the hedge-fund managers in their palatial homes offering a direct contrast to the humbler surroundings of Keith and the other hobby traders who are following him.

The gate ... and now for the fireworks

For our willing chosen ones, once they have understood what the match is that they need and how to light it, they must discover the place that will act as the tinderbox or kindling that will set the whole place ablaze. A lazy writer will simply see this as the final showdown between the chosen one and the wolf; however, this moment should be so much more than the clashing of ideologies until one has prevailed over the other. These moments are at their best when a chosen one has an emotional, psychological and spiritual connection to the challenge that is at hand. Sequences such as the final light-sabre duel in *Star Wars: Episode VI – The Return of the Jedi* (1983) are a perfect example of how to deliver these types of moments in emotionally affecting ways. They will then use the match that they have uncovered within the dark forest to finally set the world ablaze and uncover the second answer to the question they have pondering since the beginning of the film: 'What can I do to fix this?'

With *Star Wars: Episode VI – The Return of the Jedi*, Luke refuses to strike Darth Vader down as the Emperor implores him to, showing his father mercy instead. His mastery of the Force and the refusal to turn to the dark side are the match that Luke has been searching for this whole time and will be the things that see the wolf of the narrative defeated once and for all. Luke is no longer the glory-seeking farm boy from the beginning of the earlier episode. He is now a hero with morals and responsibilities, and upon his shoulders great responsibility lies.

Sarah in *Help* delivers a pitch-perfect monologue in the back of the police car, raging at the systems that have failed her and those she was caring for during the COVID-19 pandemic. She doesn't stop there and breaks the fourth wall to address us watching on, ensuring that we don't turn a blind eye to other social injustices within British society.

Although slightly beyond the scope of this title as it ultimately happens within Act 5, after the dark forest has been burnt, the chosen one is typically reminded of their special status as an outsider. They do not belong in this new world that will rise from the ashes of what they have destroyed, and it will need another chosen one to ensure that it is rebuilt. The group of samurai from *Seven Samurai* represent the old way and must return to wander Japan looking for the next village that needs their help. The one that they have saved must now be left alone to heal and grow without the violence of their existence. Other examples, such as Ethan Edwards in *The Searchers* (1956) and the drifter gunslinger looking out for the settlers in *Shane* (1953), have similar endings for their respective chosen ones.

In *The Searchers*, John Wayne's Ethan Edwards, following his battle to return his nieces from the Comanche, lingers at the door to the homestead after returning Debbie to safety. Unable to cross the threshold into civilization, he returns to the Wild West where he belongs. Although these individuals understand their place within the diegesis, you still sense that they have a longing to stay within this space that they could now call once upon a time. It is the perfect way to bring an audience to tears. Ensure in a moment like this that we feel that the chosen one has the desire to insert themselves into the new version of once upon a time they have built but the foresight to understand that they have no place within it.

A gentler version of this ending exists within more modern interpretations of this narrative where our chosen one, realizing that this time their journey is completed, now gather the allies who still have the appetite for adventure and ride off into the sunset in search of another wrong that needs righting. *Rebel Moon* is a clear example of this where our newly assembled team, who have galvanized around chosen one Kora, heads off into their next adventure in the sequel *Rebel Moon – Part Two: The Scargiver* (2024).

The wolf: I'll huff, and I'll puff …

The wolf within the willing paradigm is the most clearly defined as the entity that has either built or maintains the dark forest through which the chosen one is journeying. Every step they take within the narrative is to try and thwart the progress that our chosen one tries to make on their journey. Importantly the deck is always loaded in favour of the wolf. They know every inch of this space that they have cultivated to their own desires and are able to bend it to their will simply with a snap of their fingers.

Just like our chosen one, they will not act alone and will have their own version of a team that they have assembled around them. These surrogates are characters that they will release into the narrative at the most opportune moment to disrupt the plans that our chosen one has hatched. Using this approach to the construction of your narrative design will ensure that the obstacles you are placing in the path of your chosen one arrive at the most dramatically satisfying moment. Your chosen one will have to stretch themselves physically, emotionally, psychologically and then spiritually as the structure of the acts dictates that they should.

Unless your chosen one and the wolf have crossed paths before (more than likely in a previous narrative), they will be unknown to your wolf. Initially it may be that they are dismissive of this 'underdog' who is set on a collision course with them. However, as the wolf's awareness of them grows, they will begin to see the challenge that the chosen one brings to the established order and must start to take them seriously.

Importantly as they begin to understand more about our chosen one, the wolf realizes that the greatest way to hurt them is to separate them from their own team that they are building around them. They will try everything to knock them off course through threats and coercion or even try to tempt them from the path by appealing to their ego. Ultimately, however, it will be the prospect of harm coming to those they have gathered in the dark forest that will be too much to bear, and the wolf and chosen one will finally have to enter into the final showdown together.

Suit of armour: 'I know what I'm doing'

Initially, our chosen one arrives in the dark forest with nothing but their wits. They possess a particular set of skills that means they are suitably adept to survive or even thrive within the outer reaches of the dark forest, but they won't be able to get far without training themselves to take on the unique challenges that are in front of them on their route to retrieving the match that will burn the forest. En route, they will gather the armour they need to protect themselves against the wolf and learn how to wear it. Without showcasing any physical exertion, there will be no stakes during the final confrontation with the wolf; however, it is the team that the chosen one gathers around them that allows them to see the weaknesses they have and offer complementary strengths that will assist them in overcoming some of the darkest challenges that they face. Often these are the chosen ones that have deliberately separated themselves from a community within the opening act of the piece and they have to understand the strength that comes with camaraderie and group effort.

In Pixar's study of teenage angst, *Inside Out 2* (2024), Joy is less neurotic about Riley being blissfully happy all of the time, but she still needs to learn to relinquish control of the console at Headquarters when Riley doesn't need her. Captain Miller is evidently a good solider and a natural leader of men in *Saving Private Ryan*; however, he is unable to fully give himself over to the men he commands and is secretly just as terrified as all the others. Kora has deliberately separated herself from her community in *Rebel Moon* as she fears that in revealing her identity she will become a target of the malevolent forces searching for her.

As your chosen one discovers their suit of armour and learns how to wear it, once again the answer to the question 'How can I fix this?' will change. Consider the protection that your chosen one will need to defeat the wolf and burn the forest and then consider how this protection will make them reassess their own nature. They began your story considering themselves entirely capable of defeating the wolf but have to adopt a suit of armour as the story progresses when they realize that the person they were in Act 1 was not strong enough, capable enough or wily enough to complete the challenge before them.

Exercises

Our guest tonight is …

After all of the heroics that our chosen one has been through, it is clear that there is going to be some press attention on them. What would be the opening monologue that they would deliver for the evening? It could be an SNL experience where they have something that they have to deliver themselves … something that is written for them (how do they feel about delivering it?) or something that is delivered to welcome them onto the stage. Each of these is an exercise that would showcase a different facet of their personality.

Furthering this exercise: What are the questions that the host asks them? More importantly, what are the questions that the host doesn't ask them? These are the really juicy bits … Remember that questions invite agency from your chosen one. What are they going to do to ensure that they are not staying static and showcasing their character through the choices that they make?

Dear diary, today we had such an adventure

Have one of the allies that your chosen one has gathered around them write an entry in their diary during the downtime they have inside the dark forest. They should write explicitly about the relationship they have with the chosen one and how their specific skills match up with the lack within the chosen one, and also about some of their observations after a particularly emotional exchange while they were off the path.

In a world where ...

Write the trailer for your willing narrative. With a story on this pathway, it's always good to think about the spectacle that an audience is going to see on the screen, and there's no better place to whet their appetite than in the trailer. Think about the images and then the voice-over that is going to accompany them. How do they demonstrate the larger set pieces of the show and outline the tone of the piece?

3
Unknowing

Figure 3 *Your unknowing chosen one will have to negotiate two gates to navigate their journey.*

The unknowing chosen one makes a deal. That is the invitation in all of these narratives; that is the way that you will be able to identify an unknowing story pathway; and that is the kicking-off point for your own unknowing narrative. As we discovered in our first book, there are all kinds of ramifications to this moment of decision, and the construction of the contract made and the way that this inherently unfair deal is done will lead to the set-up of your own dark forest and prepare the way for the narrative lying before your chosen one. So, consider the deal carefully.

Since these narratives require a bargain to initiate the moment of invitation, there is often an extended preamble before the deal is proposed. We are on page 16 of the screenplay for *Jojo Rabbit* (2019) before he wakes up in the hospital following his accident with the grenade. The Jojo who emerges as he comes to consciousness, scarred and unable to join his beloved Hitler Youth, is the Jojo who will make the deal with Elsa in the attic. These stories must not only place our chosen one within their once upon a time, a set-up familiar to all screenwriters, but must also introduce a disruptor who will enter their once upon a time in order to tempt them to sign said deal. There will, therefore, be two narratives at play from the moment that upsets the chosen one's once upon a time: the chosen one's established pathway which they are set upon achieving, upset by the disruptor's pathway which sets them on a seemingly temporary diversion. In the case of *Jojo Rabbit*, this would be Jojo's set path to become a trusted member of the Nazi elite and Elsa's set path of hiding away in order to survive the war. We go into a great deal of detail about this film in our first book so if you are interested in a full breakdown of the film please refer to that.

What is at the heart of the unknowing narrative?

The unknowing storyline takes a capable chosen one away from their planned journey through life and, with the intervention of a disruptor, gives them a job to do. The dark forest appears small, the path is short, and the gate is clearly visible. However, the unique element that you will need to include in your unknowing story is that there are two gates, and this, the first gate, provides a false ending to our chosen one's journey. Just as they believe they have completed the terms of the deal, the gate opens to reveal a much larger, more dangerous, dark forest beyond and a second gate far, far in the distance.

Guy Ritchie's *The Covenant* (2023) plays fast and loose with the unknowing story arc, but all the elements are there. To all intents and purposes, this is two separate films: the story of a military mission that goes wrong and the subsequent story of a quest to save a man deep in enemy territory; however, each of these stories is initiated by one deal; when Ahmed Abdullah, an interpreter, takes on the job of working with US Special Forces Master Sergeant John Kinley in Afghanistan. The first hour of the film takes us into the world of the Special Forces' mission in Afghanistan, which ultimately ends in a disastrous mission from which Kinley escapes and Abdullah does not. The injured Kinley is flown home, and, as far as he is concerned, he has exited the story through his gate.

At the moment when our chosen one accepts the invitation in the unknowing paradigm, they have agreed to an unbalanced deal; they just don't currently know it. They have often done this for selfish or naive reasons, simply to get out of the current predicament they are in. The question that they ask themselves at the invitation and the last throw of the dice is, 'How do I get out of this?' At the outset, they are only trying to get out of the situation that they are in and take the deal for selfish reasons in the hope that it will solve the immediate problem they have before them. However, as the narrative progresses, they realize the unfair nature of the deal they first agreed to, and the meaning of the question changes with them now trying to get out of the deal they first agreed to until, at the last throw of the dice, they are finally able to work out the answer to this question. This is them undoing the deal and accepting that the reasons they had for first accepting the bargain are not representative of the new person they have now become.

With the profoundly meta *The Unbearable Weight of Massive Talent* (2022), a down-on-his-luck Nick Cage (played by Nicolas Cage) accepts the offer to become, for $1 million, the guest of honour at a billionaire superfan's birthday party. However, Nick soon becomes embroiled in a kidnapping plot that requires him to become a real-life hero and save the day.

The first gate: The road to nowhere

As we now know, the unknowing story pathway always involves two gates. The reaching and unlocking of the first gate is achieved without a key, but the opening of the gate reveals that there is a key and there is a second gate, often much more difficult to reach, which must be reached and opened before the story will be completed.

If there are two gates, then it follows that there are two paths. The first path in *The Covenant*, as with all narratives on the unknowing story arc, is a familiar one to the chosen one. Kinley's job is to seek out locations storing explosives in Afghanistan, and he's not having any luck. Ahmed is able to point him in the direction of a real IED factory, but the results are disastrous. The path, however, is clear. The team's job is to find IEDs. They learn where the IEDs are. They attempt to find them. How hard can it be?

In *The Silence of the Lambs* (1991), Agent Starling does a deal with Agent Crawford to interview the murderer and cannibal Hannibal Lecter in order to find out as much as they can about a serial killer – Buffalo Bill – who is on the loose. The path, once again, is clear. Hannibal Lecter has information, and she has ambition. What could go wrong? In *Pretty Woman* (1990), rich businessman Edward Lewis hires struggling prostitute Vivian Ward to pose as his girlfriend for a week in order to secure a business deal. The path is clear. Vivan wants Edward's money. Edward thinks that Vivian will be an asset to him in securing the lucrative deal. Both characters are acting entirely in their own self-interest. What do they have to lose?

In each of these films, our chosen ones have a clear vision of the gate and how to reach it. Kinley must discover IEDs and destroy them with the help of Ahmed; Starling must find information about Buffalo Bill with the help of Lecter; and Edward wants to secure the business deal with the help of Vivian.

In each of these cases, the gate is reached, not necessarily easily, but at least without a particular element of surprise. Ahmed is able to lead Kinley's team to a genuine Taliban bomb factory – something they have been seeking for some time. Ahmed comes through, and the team's expectations are met, but Taliban forces quickly overwhelm them, and they are decimated. Hunted through the Afghan hinterlands, Kinley is badly injured, and Ahmed displays superhuman persistence and willpower in returning him to a place of safety. Kinley is hospitalized and, shortly thereafter, returned home to the USA. His task is completed. He is a hero. He has passed through the gate.

The Silence of the Lambs is replete with false deals. The deal Starling originally makes with Crawford is followed up by a further fake deal offered by Crawford through Starling, but the central deal at play here is the one between Starling and Lecter. If she reveals personal information about herself then he will provide information that will help her identify Buffalo Bill. This he does when she tells him about her recurring nightmares. At the first gate, Starling is in possession of all the clues that will lead her to the identification of the serial killer. To all intents and purposes, her task is complete as the FBI take over … but there is another gate to reach before the killer is discovered.

In *Pretty Woman*, after a few hiccups, Vivian does her job perfectly, but Edward's business deal does not go through – not through any fault of hers but because Edward wants to break up a beloved company. Here, at the first gate, following the completion of the deal, weaknesses in Edward's character are revealed. He clearly has a lesson to learn before he can exit this story to his, and our, satisfaction.

In each of these cases, our chosen ones have completed the deal and arrived at the gate, but the film is not over. This moment very often happens around two-thirds of the way through the film, and it represents a moment of realization for our chosen ones. The belief that by completing the deal they would be satisfied and able to return to their once upon a time is dispelled. The gate is too easily reached. There is no key, and it just swings open freely, but what it reveals beyond is not the comfort and security of home but, rather, a second path leading to a second gate, much further away, much more securely locked and in need of a key to open it.

As you construct your unknowing storyline, consider the roles of your chosen one and your disruptor. The disruptor must have a clear goal which, in their minds, can only be reached if they persuade the chosen one to get on board, but either they do not inform the chosen one of all the facts or the task they have set is much more difficult than either of them at first imagined. You have to develop two clear, complex characters here, both asking themselves, 'How do I get out of this?' The chosen one will answer that they are a person who has decided to help out another for personal reward or philanthropic reasons, and, when the deal is complete, they will simply leave the narrative and continue where they left off. The disruptor will keep their answer close to their chests. They may say, 'I'm someone who needs help in order to get out of trouble', but the type of help they need will not be fully expressed in the deal made with the chosen one, and the trouble will prove much more difficult to resolve.

The key: Hidden deep within

The key to the second gate is only discoverable after the first gate has been opened, and the whereabouts of the key is in the changed character of the chosen one. Despite the relative ease with which the first gate is reached, in travelling the path with the disruptor, something fundamental will have changed within the chosen one that will force them to look deep within themselves to further embrace that change and approach the second gate as a chosen one driven by an entirely new set of wants and needs. Here, the answer to the question. 'How do I get out of this?' will be fundamentally different from the answer given in Act 1.

In *The Covenant*, Kinley would not be alive and home without Ahmed, who is now on the run from the Taliban with a wife and baby. He is in mortal fear for his life, and Kinley's perspective on the world has changed. He is not content. He can't sleep. He has a debt that must be repaid. The super-confident master sergeant used to delivering orders and unhappy if those orders are challenged is replaced by a man driven by a moral imperative. Kinley's tour of duty is over. He doesn't have to return to Afghanistan and put himself in danger for another man, but he is impelled to do so by the debt he owes.

In *The Silence of the Lambs*, Starling has been forced to look deep within herself by Lecter. She doesn't have to go to Gumb's house to try to rescue Catherine; that's the FBI's job. However, she is compelled to act by the traumatic memory of slaughtered lambs. Catherine's fate is tied inextricably together with her trauma, and, in order to rid herself of her nightmares, Starling must put herself in danger to rescue Catherine.

In *Pretty Woman*, Edward has paid Vivian. Their deal is over and done with, but, even though it will take him a while to admit it, Vivian and he have connected on a much deeper level. If Edward is going to emerge from this story as a better person, he is going to have to stop paying for his pleasures with money and start paying with truth, honesty and humility – the polar opposite of the Edward we have come to know.

Off the path: Lost in the dark with no map

In each of these examples, our chosen ones have already trodden the path. They have done their deals and fulfilled their duties in order to reach the gate. On the other side of the first gate, however, the path is obscure, covered in weeds and difficult to find. Everything from here on in is off the path. The second gate is hidden deep in the dark forest, and they must negotiate unfamiliar territory without map or compass to reach it. They are in possession of the key to open it, but it will take them a while to realize this.

Kinley's return to Afghanistan is decidedly at odds with his first appearance there. As a master sergeant, Kinley was in charge and used to being obeyed by his team. When he returns under the pseudonym, Ron Kay, he is ostensibly a nobody who has paid for the services of private military contractor, Parker. He is in the hands of others now, and others are about to thrust him even further into the dark forest as Parker reneges on his agreement with Kay/Kinley to aid him in the rescue. Kay/Kinley heads into enemy territory with no support, driven by his need to rescue Ahmed. He is now the most wanted man in Afghanistan, and it won't take long for the Taliban to discover that he is back.

Starling's decision to follow her hunch in tracking down Jame Gumb is similarly driven by her internal psychological need. Her arrival at Gumb's house will find her thrust into, literally, the darkest of dark forests as Gumb stalks her through the pitch-black building wearing night vision goggles.

Edward's diversion off the path, in keeping with a light romantic comedy, is less outwardly traumatic for him but no less effective in placing him in unfamiliar, uncomfortable territory as he seeks to come to terms with his own psychological imperative. His various attempts to keep Vivian close to him fail because he continues to act by exerting power and control rather being true to his own nature.

Once again, we find these unknowing narratives replete with attempted deals and bargains as the stories unfold. As Parker reneges on his deal with Kay/Kinley, our chosen one yells, 'I want you to honour the fucking deal!' As Kinley reflects on the US Army's withdrawal from Afghanistan, he states, 'The deal was that we offered his family sanctuary, then we tied a noose around his neck and kicked the stool out from under him.' Just as Edward's deal with Kross develops and changes as he develops and changes, so he keeps trying to renegotiate his deal with Vivian until he realizes that a deal will no longer do it. It takes Vivian to teach him that not everything has to be a deal. When he points out to Vivian that 'I'm getting a lecture on ethics from a prostitute', she responds, 'at least there are some things I won't do for money.' Deals aren't always the answer to a happy life, and these narratives are continually reminding us that honesty and self-reflection have more lasting value than the *quid pro quo* of Hannibal Lecter's association with Agent Starling.

The wolf: The sheep's clothing is gone

There are wolves aplenty in these wheeler-dealer narratives, but the true nature of the wolf is only revealed after the first gate has been breached. What had appeared as a relatively simple arrangement becomes more complex as the expected ending becomes just another step along the way to a conclusion that will require the chosen one to dig deep and expose themselves emotionally to the process. Here is where the wolf comes into their own, deep in the dark forest on the far side of the first gate, a fearsome antagonist.

In *The Covenant*, when Kinley returns to Afghanistan, he has been divested of his army rank and military support. The wolf is the amorphous, ever-present, ever-vigilant presence of the Taliban who, following their humiliation at Kinley and Ahmed's escape, have placed them both at the top of their most wanted list.

What was, prior to the arrival at the first gate, a ragtag band of fairly incompetent militiamen is now a well-connected army with eyes everywhere and a clear command structure. When Kinley is spotted on the road, word travels quickly through the ranks of the Taliban, and their seemingly invincible forces move in to cut off their escape.

The wolf, in *The Silence of the Lambs*, is not Hannibal Lecter. Lecter is Starling's disruptor and holds no physical threat to her. Emotional, yes; physical, no. The wolf, in the form of Buffalo Bill, is waiting in the wings throughout the journey to the first gate but is not revealed to her as the insane tailor Jame Gumb until after Starling has entered the world off the path beyond the first gate.

Crucially, Gumb does not know of Starling and her search for him until the final showdown at his house. Similarly to the Taliban in *The Covenant*, Gumb only reacts to the presence of the chosen one rather than seeking them out. The final showdown takes place in the wolf's lair, just as the final showdown in *The Covenant* takes place deep in Taliban territory. In both cases, the wolf is wily and powerful and is only defeated through the cunning, skill and training of our chosen one, alongside a modicum of good luck.

While *Pretty Woman* is a very different film dealing with a very different kind of wolf, many of the same rules apply to the journey off the path for

Edward. The journey to the first gate sees Edward behaving as expected: establishing a deal, conforming to the parameters of the deal and fulfilling the expectations of the deal to the best of his ability. Vivian, however, is a prime example of a disruptor, and not only does she witness the failure of Edward's deal with Kross, she is also able to act as moral arbiter for the failed takeover and reveal to Edward his own shortcomings in an unexpected way.

As they enter the world off the path beyond the first gate, Edward's compass is off. He knows that he wants Vivian but doesn't know how to achieve that aim. The wolf is essentially the world's view of Vivian as a prostitute to which Edward, initially at least, conforms. Vivian is a strong, independent woman who makes her own choices, one of which is to work as a prostitute, and when she falls for Edward it will not be possible for them to become a couple unless his world view is fundamentally changed.

The world view that sees Vivian, a prostitute, as not worthy of a normal, happy life with the man she loves is embodied at a crucial moment in the story by Edward's lawyer, Philip. Philip is aware of Vivian's job and also jealous of her influence over Edward. When he hits her and attempts to rape her, it is the catalyst that Edward needs to begin the process of real change. The world's view of prostitution as being outside of acceptable society is successfully challenged when Edward fires Philip, and this moment sets him on track for a re-evaluation of his own world view. The world's view of prostitution does not become an issue and therefore is not an effective wolf until Edward has passed through the first gate and fallen for Vivian, and Philip is not needed as a personification of that world view until the moment is right for Edward's conflicted nature to be challenged.

The suit of armour: The wrong trousers

Each of the chosen ones we have discussed in this chapter has a clear and obvious suit of armour associated with their professional lives. Kinley wears military fatigues. Starling wears, first, an FBI branded sweatshirt and afterwards a functional, grey FBI suit. Edward wears expensive suits and dresses Vivian up to match. Outwardly, their uniforms embed them in the worlds from which the story will have them emerge.

The unknowing chosen one is wearing the wrong suit of armour. During the course of the story, they will typically divest themselves of this clothing as they realize that it is suffocating them. The suit of armour, though, is not only the clothes that represent them, it is also the chosen one's perspective on the world. Their suit of armour is a shield, hiding their true selves from the world outside and stopping them from realizing their full potential.

Dressed in his military fatigues, Kinley is a capable and professional soldier, but he is ultimately a failure. His attempts to discover IEDs in Afghanistan results in his team getting wiped out by the Taliban, him getting injured and, with his military clothing removed, transported to safety by, on the face of it, the least crucial member of his unit. Psychologically, he is a soldier through and through, driven by a need to find explosives, and he will bend the rules to this end. However, this journey will reveal to him that people are more valuable than explosives.

Dressed in her professional uniform, Starling is an ambitious trainee and keen to progress up the ranks of the FBI. Psychologically, the course of the journey from the first to the second gate will reveal to her that the rulebook that governs the behaviour of the textbook FBI operative must be ignored or subverted in order to gain results. Despite being told explicitly not to divulge personal information to Lecter, she does so. Despite Crawford taking the case off her hands when she discovers the true identity of Buffalo Bill, she continues to pursue him. During the course of the story, Starling throws off her identity as a trainee and adopts the persona of a fully fledged FBI operative. She will have to participate in Thomas Harris's follow-up story, *Hannibal*, so the FBI is her home for the time being. By the time Lecter has finished disrupting her life in *Hannibal*, her original suit of armour will be well and truly gone.

Dressed in his expensive suits, Edward exudes confidence and business acumen. He is as absolutely at home in this environment as Kinley is in his, but the integrity of this environment will be slowly eroded by Vivian as the film progresses. While Edward physically never really breaks away from his image as a powerful and successful businessman, Vivian's dream of a knight on a white steed is realized by him in the final scenes as he climbs his way to her apartment. These are not the actions of a corporate businessman. Edward is briefly but effectively transformed into a romantic knight, shedding his psychological suit of armour as he adopts Vivian's fairy-tale vision of a hero who will save her from her life and transport her to a better place.

The second gate: Summon up the strength from within

As our chosen ones approach the second gate, their suits of armour will be falling away, and the wolves will be closing in. The job of the writer here is to clearly identify the key that will allow the chosen one to exit the second gate and complete the narrative.

As we have seen, the key and the wolf are only really identifiable following the arrival at the first gate. The journey to the first gate establishes the conflicted nature of the chosen one and, by passing through that gate, that conflicted nature is laid bare both for themselves and for others.

As you write your unknowing storyline, the requirements of the narrative become clear when you begin to reflect on other films that employ this dramatic arc. Your chosen one must not only accept a deal before they enter the dark forest; they must also be set in their ways. They must be set on a pathway in life that does not fit their essential character. A military officer hidebound by rules must learn to act outside of the rules because it is the right thing to do. An FBI trainee must forget her training and go by instinct in order to really be effective in her chosen profession. A successful corporate businessman must sacrifice money for morality if he truly wants to be happy. The repeated question of 'How do I get out of this?' will probably gain the most different answers of all of our pathways as the journey progresses through the dark forest because each path and each gate requires fundamental change, and the key will see that change enacted.

When you set up your chosen one, consider who they are at the beginning of the story and who you want them to be by the end, then make those two things as far apart as you can possibly imagine them to be. Crucially, your chosen one should not know that they are in need of a change. They believe that they are set on the correct course in their lives. It will take the arrival of the disruptor to upset the balance of their individual narrative. The story of a poor street hustler who ends up making a killing on Wall Street as a market trader (*Trading Places*, 1983) and the story of a respectable vice president of a media corporation who ends making a fortune as a successful criminal (*Fun with Dick and Jane*, 2005) are both examples of rags-to-riches stories based on a deal that has unexpected consequences.

At the heart of the unknowing story arc there is a chosen one who needs to change but doesn't yet realize it, and it is important to note that neither the rags, nor the riches, are central to the conceit. One of the most famous unknowing storylines of all time sees the unhappy, disillusioned George Bailey do a deal with an angel following a lengthy introduction to his life and history. *It's a Wonderful Life* (1946), as with other films following this pathway, is full of deals as George attempts to keep his father's business, a building and loan, open, as he gives his university tuition fees to his younger brother on the proviso that he take over the company following his studies, and as he and his new wife use their savings to shore up the company. There are also deals that go nowhere as George attempts to appease the loathsome Mr Potter. Ultimately, however, it is the deal he does with his trainee guardian angel, Clarence, that reveals his true worth to himself, his family and his community.

The real value of the unknowing storyline is in having a character divert, albeit unwillingly, from their set path in life, but for that diversion to be the very thing that alters their life, generally for the better. The unknowing story is rich with depth and psychological possibility. The storyline lends itself to great highs and deep lows, and the particular way in which the key elements of the story – the path, the gate, the key, off the path, the wolf, the suit of armour and, crucially and uniquely to this storyline, the second gate – work together to send your chosen one on an unexpected and enriching story means that many of these narratives remain enduringly popular with audiences.

Exercises

Lie-detector test

Used in interrogation scenes across the canon of film and TV, the lie-detector-test sequence is a great way for writers to really show off their dialogue-writing skills. Within the questions and answers there is a huge amount of subtext that showcases how the character relates to the dark forest they are in and the inner journey that they are on. Strap your unknowing chosen one up to a polygraph machine and have them answer a series of questions that are put to them by another character. What is it that they lie about? What do they allow themselves to admit? How do they react when they are called out or not called out for their untruths?

As within the other paradigms, when creating sequences like this, try and focus on the specific part of the journey that your chosen one is on at the point when the test is administered. How far they are through the dark forest will obviously dictate how they respond to the questions as they are less/more aware of their need to change. For questions that might really help you dig into the core mechanics of the paradigm, it would be good to focus on the initial deal into which your chosen one has entered and their motivations for agreeing to it.

Great examples of this scene include *Meet the Parents* (2000) where Greg is probed by his prospective father-in-law while he is hooked up to a lie detector in the basement of his house, with hilarious results. For a different tonal experience of the same sort of scene, look at *BlacKkKlansman* (2018) where Flip Zimmerman arrives in another basement with a Klansman who is insistent that he take a lie-detector test that would unravel the entire operation that Flip and Ron have worked so hard on. Flip manages to avoid being strapped into the machine but still is harshly interrogated by the man opposite him. Finally, although not strictly a lie-detector scene, *The Master* (2012) sees our chosen one Freddie Quell probed by Lancaster Dodd during 'processing' that is supposed to help Quell understand himself better. In the beginning, our chosen one mocks the process but after embracing it ends up unlocking a powerful memory that assists him in understanding a deep and painful truth he has been holding back all this time.

DVD cover art

Although streaming has entirely disrupted the film industry as we know it, there are still some of us out there who like to own the physical copy of the media that we consume. (Yes ... the audio commentaries are worth it ...) The cover art also helps to position the piece both tonally and within the broader genre to which it belongs. For your film, create the DVD box art that you think best communicates your overall vision for the piece. If you are confident with a program like Photoshop, fire that up and get creating, but sometimes simply sketching down your ideas can give you an indication of the work that you would like to create. It might also be good to explore your ideas in some of the AI image-generation tools that you have at your disposal. Even though they produce imperfect results, sometimes they can create an interesting image for you to develop further.

If you are wanting to expand on this exercise, you might want to think about developing the 'limited edition' SteelBook edition for your piece and how that might be different from your initial release.

Emoji film

In keeping with the mantra *Simple story, complex characters*, showcase the plot of your narrative using only emojis. What is the string of graphics that you can type out on your phone that would best express the narrative that you are trying to tell? Start using the five that represent the respective acts of the piece and then go deeper into the sequences, then the scenes and finally, if you are so inclined, the beats of the piece you are writing.

4
Unable to believe

Figure 4 *The unable to believe chosen one must come to appreciate the armour they have.*

Every hero has to start somewhere. The story of an underdog surviving and then thriving when everything is stacked against them is the staple arc of any decent origin story. In these narratives, the unlikeliest of all chosen ones are plucked from obscurity by a mentor (or tormentor) who believes in them enough to guide them through a journey that will see them transform from ugly duckling to majestic swan.

Often this arc lends itself very well to the shape of biopics or sports films. However, it can also be a paradigm that allows for you to effectively write a quest or a road movie where our chosen one accepts an invitation where they come to discover that it's the journey not the destination that is important. These narratives can be as diverse in tone and stakes as *The Lord of the Rings: The Fellowship of the Ring* (2001) and *Little Miss Sunshine* (2006). Both of these experiences feel just as important to the characters in them as they head off on their respective adventures. Just because they are not saving *the* world doesn't mean that they aren't saving *their* world.

In these narratives, you will need to create a chosen one who is worthy but they don't quite realize this yet or have determined that they are not worthy at all. They will discover the worth inside themselves through their experience in the dark forest and then in the end celebrate with those who helped them and vanquish those who doubted or opposed them. It is through the chosen one's interactions with their (tor)mentor that they experience the profound realization that they are worth more than the version of them we first met in their once upon a time. The initial answer to the question, 'Who am I?' will therefore be clear and concise: 'I am unworthy.' The entire narrative is working towards the opposite answer to this question when they emerge as a swan: 'I am now worthy.'

The specific question that they come to ask of themselves is an existential one that seems right for the paradigm that has a chosen one who is more often than not constantly questioning every step they take along the path with their (tor)mentor. Their question is, 'Who am I meant to be?'

The vertigo-inducing *Fall* (2022) has free climber Becky begin the piece in a once upon a time where she is an alcoholic shut in after the death of her husband in a climbing accident. The answer to, 'Who am I meant to be?', is a bleak one where she believes she is literally at the verge of contemplating dying by suicide. It takes her best friend and mentor, Hunter, to invite her to climb a decommissioned TV tower in the desert to snap her out of her depression and get her climbing again. However, when the ladder that is the only way down from the tower breaks, the pair are trapped 2,000 feet in the air. As the more confident of the two, Hunter continues to encourage Becky to survive despite things looking dire. During the last throw of the dice, Becky is able to find the strength inside her to finally do what needs to be done to ensure that she can get off the platform in the sky. Without the mentorship of Hunter, she would long ago have given up on being able to get down. Her journey is one that takes her on the most dramaturgically and dramatically satisfying arc from one extreme (death) to the other (survival).

What is at the heart of the unable-to-believe narrative?

As every reader of this book (or our previous book) is very aware by now, character is structure. Nowhere is this more overt than within the unable-to-believe narrative, where the dark forest is one that is inside the chosen one. They are a character who is fundamentally at war with themselves and are unable to see the greatness that they possess in whatever skill their (tor)mentor is trying to get them to see. These are the narratives of (wo)man against themselves. It may be that the external dark forest that they are within is a hostile one to them, but the densest and darkest one that they have to journey through is that which they have built within their own minds.

The relationship that you construct between the (tor)mentor and their chosen one is key to establishing the overarching tone and theme of the piece that you are writing, and this is the unique element we find in the unable-to-believe story arc. Ultimately, Daniel LaRusso is nothing without Mr Miyagi in *The Karate Kid*. Luke Skywalker would remain a farmhand on Tatooine without Obi-Wan Kenobi delivering the invitation to him in *Star Wars: Episode IV – A New Hope*; and Eliza Doolittle would stay as a humble flower-seller without Professor Higgins's intervention in *My Fair Lady*.

What you are trying to communicate in your understanding of the relationship between students and teachers here is the core of the ideas you are exploring. Building the bond that (tor)mentor and mentee share more typically happens in the off-the-path scenes that you construct where your (tor)mentor is attempting to bring the chosen one back onto the path or when the pair deliberately signal that they are going to take a breather from their shared path for a moment.

It is interesting that both *The Karate Kid* and *Star Wars: Episode IV – A New Hope* offer us an inversion of the narrative arcs our chosen ones are on with their wolves themselves having tormentors who are pushing them too hard within their own dark forests. A solid contrast like this can assist in reinforcing the overall thematic ideas that you are waiting to explore in your work while also giving us a good indication of the wolf's motivations and allowing us to empathize with a character who might not initially have a plethora of redeemable qualities to them. Although we can never agree with the actions that Johnny Lawrence takes in *The Karate Kid*, we understand how he has become who he is once we have met Sensei Kreese and how he treats his young mentee.

An important mechanism to consider within these narratives is when your chosen one fully assimilates the true nature of your (tor)mentor's teachings. Often it will be that your (tor)mentor will deliver a lesson that your chosen one will not fully understand the point of or that will seem irrelevant when they first start exploring it. The most famous of these is Mr Miyagi instructing Daniel to 'paint the fence' and 'sand the floor'. The young pupil believes that this is the old man simply getting him to do some long-forgotten chores, but all becomes clear to him when he is asked to repeat the motion to deflect Miyagi's punches and kicks. It is also mostly true that the tor(mentors) within these narratives were once themselves chosen ones who journeyed through a comparable dark forest. Their attitude to their teaching methods are shaped by the experience they had while on their own journeys. This will not only allow them privileged skills and information that will assist the chosen one in growing into the swan they are destined to be but also has them understand that the ugly duckling's transformation is a process. The chosen one will have to explore more facets than simply their physical training. They will also have to develop an understanding of their emotional, psychological and spiritual relationship to themselves and the dark forest in which they are in the midst. Lionel Logue directly outlines this to Bertie in *The King's Speech* (2010) as he eventually accepts the invitation offered to him. However, at this tentative moment, Bertie has no interest in discussing why he stammers in the way he does and would rather be given exercises to improve his speech mechanics. The acceptance that maybe there are some other reasons for his speech disorder only comes much later when he is ready to process this with Lionel by his side.

The (tor)mentor: 'Do as I say, not as I do'

There are two versions of the figure that will guide your chosen one during their journey through the dark forest. There will be the mentors who will push, cajole and encourage your chosen one along the path. These are generous teachers who will sometimes be firm with them but who will always have their best interests at heart. The methods they use will often be unorthodox, and at times your chosen one will be uncertain how the things that they are learning will assist them on their journey. However, once they trust in the process, it will soon be clear that the skills they are gathering will be key to their success in the dark forest.

Mickey Goldmill in *Rocky* (1967) and Professor Albus Dumbledore in *Harry Potter and the Philosopher's Stone* (2001) are perfect examples of these. However, there is the tormentor who will drag, berate and belittle your chosen one into following the path that lies before them. Their teaching style will be entirely different from their kind and benevolent alter egos. They often push too hard and too fast with our chosen ones. They do see the greatness in the mentees but often see the transformation they want from them above all else often with disastrous consequences. Tyler Durden from *Fight Club* (1999) and John du Pont in *Foxcatcher* (2014) are both examples of these kinds of characters.

One of the greatest versions of this narrative paradigm is *The Karate Kid* (1984) where a young Daniel LaRusso moves with his mother from Newark, New Jersey to Reseda in Los Angeles, California. It is there that he meets his mentor, Mr Miyagi, who will teach him how to become a karate champion but will also assist the teenager in finding his feet in his new home. A more modern example of this paradigm is *The King's Speech* which simply is a must-watch for those who are attempting to navigate this structural arc. In this version of the narrative, speech therapist Lionel Logue assists the future King George VI to find his voice both literally and metaphorically during the time they spend together on screen.

For those looking to write the darker subversion of this narrative, you should certainly engage with *Whiplash* (2014), which has one of the greatest tormentor figures from modern cinema in the malevolent Terence Fletcher, which we covered extensively in our last book. However, if you can peer beyond some of the more slightly dated values in the piece, *My Fair Lady* gives a clear indication of the strained relationship between tormentor and chosen one. When Eliza Doolittle is first subjected to the teachings of Henry Higgins, who insists that he can have her speak with an upper-class accent, she even sings a full song called 'Just You Wait' about all the terrible things that she wishes she could do to him, which showcases her personal resentment at his teaching techniques and her misunderstanding of the importance that they have to developing her elocution. For a postmodern twist on the same ideas, *Fight Club* is the perfect example of how a tormentor figure delivers their lessons to a chosen one in harsh and unpleasant ways. The twist here is that tormentor and chosen one are the same person.

Suit of armour: This old thing here

The suit of armour is central to the narrative trajectory of your unable-to-believe narrative arc. Your chosen one will start with what they think is some rusty old armour that they are either ashamed of, not wanting to wear or not looking after properly. As they venture into the dark forest, they realize that once it's polished up in a joint effort between them and their (tor)mentor, it becomes strong, beautiful and something to be proud of. This is a gradual process that is central to the experience of the unable-to-believe chosen one within the dark forest and should be clearly tracked by you as you progress through your screenplay. However, it must also be evident that this chosen one has something special about them that both us in the audience and their (tor)mentor can see, an admirable quality or trait that draws us to them and allows us to see that if only the chosen one was able to build upon this they would be able to achieve greatness. Daniel in *The Karate Kid* is resilient and caring, whereas Bertie in *The King's Speech* is persistent and humble. Finally, Eliza in *My Fair Lady* is fierce and independent. All these are traits that make them not only active characters within the story but also engaging for us to watch as we root for them to succeed in their mission to realize their own greatness.

The path: You're the best around …

For our unable-to-believe chosen ones, the journey down the path towards the gate is the chance they get to finally reveal that they have been a swan this whole time. A challenge will await them at the gate, and it is up to the (tor)mentor to have the chosen one realize that they are fully ready for it.

Indeed, they might have been prepared much sooner if they were only able to see the greatness that they have within them. This will also be a special event that our chosen one will be explicitly training for, a space where they will be able to unveil their special status (and special skill) to the ones who are the most important to them. For Olive in *Little Miss Sunshine*, this is the pageant in which she will compete at the end of the family road trip. With Daniel in *The Karate Kid*, it is the 1984 All Valley Karate Tournament. In *My Fair Lady*, Eliza must pass herself off as a duchess at an embassy ball. Having a clear end in sight for the chosen one helps you to create a narrative with a simple goal that your audience will buy into. Once again, the *Simple story, complex character* formula is at the core of this element of the story.

Off the path: Nothing's gonna ever keep you down

Our unable-to-believe chosen ones are the ones who really don't want to follow the path. In fact, they are generally desperate to avoid having to go off on adventure in the first place. It is likely that they have shaped their once upon a time so that it allows them to either hide their conflicted nature or ensure that they do not have to ever confront it in a meaningful way. This is the space that your chosen one will go to so that they do not have to continue on with their journey because it is too hard for them to carry on. Once they find themselves there, they will need to be assisted by their (tor)mentor in returning to the path. It is within these moments that they will learn lessons that they will take with them back onto the path and allow them to further bolster their resolve for the trials that lie ahead. In addition, these moments will give you space as a writer to explore that all-important relationship between the mentee and (tor)mentor and allow them to strengthen the ties that hold them together. These stops along the way are often best when they are unplanned or inconvenient for the narrative trajectory of the piece and should take our chosen one gradually further and further away from the path as the story continues so that mentee and (tor)mentor must race back to the path with increasing haste. It is also interesting to see in the build-up to your chosen one arriving at the gate how much you can fracture the bond between the chosen one and (tor)mentor so that they must work to return to their previously strong relationship. These sequences allow for our chosen one and (tor)mentor to develop the relationship that they have away from the rather functional elements that will take place on the path.

In *Little Miss Sunshine*, as the family journeys on the path of their road trip, there are frequent stops that take them on adjacent adventures. One notable occasion is where Dwayne realizes that he is colour-blind and therefore will never be able to fulfil his dream of being a fighter pilot, forcing the family to pull over so that he can vent his frustrations and finally break his vow of silence. This generates a subplot within the movie where Dwayne's uncle Frank encourages the teenager to come to an understanding that, although his disappointments will hurt him, he has something special inside him. Importantly though, it allows Dwayne to better (and more vocally) support his sister as she progresses on her path towards the beauty pageant.

In *Green Book* (2019), Tony Lip and Don Shirley journey through the Midwest and Deep South of the USA in 1962 so that Don can play piano at various private events. Navigating the racism of the Jim Crow laws, Tony is hired specifically as a white man to accompany Don in the hopes that it will mean that Don will be able to complete his tour without incident. Both men learn much from each other and as a two-hander act as the mentor for the other at various points in the narrative. They are frequently dragged off the path by choice but also by circumstance. None of these moments is more obvious than when, after Tony assaults a police officer, the pair end up in a jail cell and are in danger of missing one of Don's performances. While in the cell together, Don chastises Tony for his hot-headedness, telling him that they should always face any situation with dignity. The pair are then released once Don has used his one phone call to speak to Attorney General Robert F. Kennedy. Tony then takes this lesson out onto the road with him as the pair continue onto the path. A more light-hearted example is where Don assists Tony in writing a romantic love letter to his wife who is waiting for him at home. The piece takes them no closer to the end of the path but allows for them to explore the relationship that they share with one another and how this will inform their future direction of travel.

The two examples above show a very clear delineation between the path and off the path as they are both road movies. However, it is also true of our examples where there is no physical road that our characters are on. Mr Miyagi is constantly looking out for Daniel as he tries to navigate his love triangle between him, Johnny and Ali at his high school. The elder mentor even uncovers the perfect costume for Daniel to attend his dance in so as not to attract attention. In addition, there is another scene where the pair bond in a tender moment when Daniel helps Miyagi into bed after hearing the story of his heroism during the Second World War and the death of his wife and son in childbirth. These things help them bond and allow for a greater trust and respect that assists them on further navigating their way through the path.

The gate: The rabbit out of the hat

For our unable-to-believe chosen ones, the gate is, and has always been, wide open. It is just that the chosen one has been unable to walk through it as they haven't had their (tor)mentor by their side to allow them to see the greatness inside them. It is the true embodiment of the mantra: it is the journey and not the destination. This is one of the reasons why this narrative arc works well for a road movie. Just before they are able to walk beyond the threshold of the gate in these narratives and finally reach the other side of their dark forest, our chosen ones must finally reveal themselves to have been a swan this whole time. They can only do this once they have internalized all of the lessons that the (tor)mentor has been attempting to teach them for the central two-thirds of the narrative that you are writing.

One of the best examples of this comes in *The King's Speech* where, on the eve of his coronation, Bertie has lost all confidence in Lionel and confronts him about what he believes is his 'dishonesty' about his qualifications. Lionel sets the future king straight, letting him know that there was no deception on his part and that everything he has learnt about his craft came from lived experience. It appears that mentor and chosen one have completely broken their relationship and it needs to be repaired. As Bertie turns his back feeling sorry for himself, Lionel sits on the throne, sending our chosen one into a rage that finally has him shout: 'I have a voice!', something Lionel has been trying to get his mentee to recognize from the beginning of the film. His mentor merely smiles and says, 'Yes, you do.'

The Karate Kid has a notoriously short final act showing the celebration of Daniel's success in the All Valley tournament and a freeze-frame of Mr Miyagi's smiling face. The gate through which Daniel passes is the final confrontation between him and Johnny where he is at last able to showcase a mastery of all his skills and perform the crane kick despite being hurt in the last round.

The key: 'I'm not Tyler Durden!'

The key is inside our chosen ones, but they do not have any faith that they are able to find it no matter how hard they search within themselves. This is often showcased at the gate as they are able to master the skill that they have been building towards during the piece once they have the confidence to perform it.

For Olive in *Little Miss Sunshine*, she performs her unconventional routine at the pageant free from the hang-ups of the customary performances expected of a beauty queen. Even in the description of the visuals within the screenplay you get a clear understanding that she is breaking the traditional mould of what would be expected at such an event. Without the pressures of having to win the contest, she is simply able to enjoy herself. Her infectious enthusiasm and confidence draw the rest of her family up on stage, and for a moment they are able to forget their troubles and simply live in the moment.

Tyler Durden in *Fight Club* has great plans for our narrator and the wider Project Mayhem that he creates out of his Fight Club that started in a bar basement. He bullies, belittles and hazes his charges to mould them into the men that he believes they need to be for his plans to work. His master plan is unveiled (in the Western release of the film) at the top of a tall tower as he outlines to our narrator that he will erase all of the debt records by blowing up the headquarters of credit-card companies. The narrator cannot accept this and shoots himself in the mouth, 'killing' Tyler. It is interesting to note that the Chinese release of the film cuts around this radical conclusion and has the narrator accepting professional help after ultimately foiling Tyler's plans. This change prompted criticism from both Palahniuk, as the author of the book the film is based on, and David Fincher, the director, as it was not in keeping with the broader thematic ideas of the piece. In addition, it also feels akin to the worst of all sins a writer can commit while writing an ending whereby we in the audience are made to understand, 'It was all a dream.'

The wolf: 'You're all a bunch of Daniel-sans …'

Just as the key is within our chosen one so, too is the wolf. Our chosen ones are their own worst enemy, and they are constantly trying to find ways to sabotage the progress they are making as they venture through the dark forest. Once they have let their wolf out, it falls to their (tor)mentor, generally in an off-the-path scene, to help them see the trait(s) they have just exhibited. Though there may be an external manifestation of a wolf, the real antagonism lies within them and their inability to realize their own greatness.

In *Next Goal Wins* (2023), Thomas Rongen takes over the coaching duties for the American Samoa football team who have previously suffered the worst loss in the history of the game. His path is clear. He has to shape a team of misfits into a squad that will finally score the nation's first ever goal in a competitive game. This is hindered by the past trauma of the death of his daughter that he is holding onto and masking with alcohol abuse. It falls to a fa'afafine player on the team, Jaiyah Saelua, to assist the coach to see beyond his belief that he is an ugly duckling when they meet off the path, just as it is Thomas's job to assist Jaiyah in finding her greatness on the pitch. However, due to his traumatic past with his daughter, who Jaiyah reminds him of, he treats her unfairly when they first meet. This is an example of the chosen one allowing the wolf inside them to take over just when they should be moving along the path towards the gate and their destiny as a swan. Their relationship comes to a head in the locker room just before the big game at the end where they can confide in one another one last time off the path and showcase the growth they have both been through during the adventure they went on together. The piece is stuffed full of clever economical writing in that it frequently references other famous unable-to-believe sports films that share a similar structural and tonal DNA.

There are nods to *The Karate Kid*, *The Mighty Ducks* (1992) and even *Any Given Sunday* (1999) throughout that occur at similar structural moments within those films. It even manages a reference to *The Matrix* (1999), where Thomas is compared to Neo as a very overt indication of his status as the chosen one.

This is the last chance for your chosen one to ask themselves the question, 'Who am I meant to be?' The answer your chosen one gives at this point will reveal how far your journey has taken them. If the answer they give is too similar to the one that they provided at the beginning of the story, then you will have to dig a little deeper to really get to the heart of what your story is about. The chosen one who emerges as a swan at the end of this story should be as diametrically opposed in terms of self-belief and overt ability to the ugly duckling we met at the beginning of your screenplay as it is possible to be.

Exercises

'What I'm looking for in a partner …'

Your unable-to-believe chosen one isn't the type who would traditionally put themselves out there; however, you're going to create a dating profile for them so they can start looking for their next romantic connection. Imagine them well before their (tor)mentor has come into their lives so this is them at peak ugly duckling.

You can tackle this exercise from a twenty-first-century perspective and set them up on one of the apps. They'll need a catchy and snappy bio that reveals them to the world and lets everyone know what they are looking for. However, these aren't the characters who are used to this sort of behaviour, and it may be that they are leaving in a little of their true feelings about themselves and within the subtext we can tell that they aren't all that comfortable doing this. You could further this idea by mocking up how you think the first few interactions they have with their initial matches might go. These could be horrible, humorous or entirely honest (maybe a little too honest).

It might be fun to give the exercise a historic twist where you have your chosen one record a to-camera tape for an old-school dating agency where they answer a series of set questions on camera. You can decide what these are, but examples could be the basics like, 'What makes you laugh?' 'What are you looking for in a partner?' 'What do you do for fun?' Innocuous enough, but how can your chosen one's answers hint at that status they acutely feel as an ugly duckling. Remember that they are being recorded so they are being the version of them that they want to try and project to the world but frequently are letting stuff slip by that they didn't mean to.

Build them a treehouse

As we have discussed above, the chosen ones in this narrative arc are forever running off from the path and must be brought back to continue on their journey. As part of this exercise, you are going to create the description of the (metaphorical or otherwise) space that your chosen one is heading for. Importantly, what is it that this space represents about your chosen one's conflicted nature and how does it reflect the old life that they have left behind to go on this journey?

Write the detailed scene description of this space as a starting point. To challenge yourself a little more, it would be good to write a short hypothetical scene where your character encounters this space. Think about how they would move about this environment. What is it that they pick up or put down? How do they eventually leave, and what are they determined to do once they have closed the door and descended the ladder?

Mindless scrolling

Our social-media algorithms are frightening things. Often, they reveal a little too much about our search history for comfort with retargeted ads based on the last things we were typing (terrifying for a writer penning something about serial killers – 'how to hide body effectively' was just for research, I swear.)

Park your chosen one down in the middle of the narrative that you have written and have them get out their phone. For those of you who are writing a piece where these things don't exist, it's time to get anachronistic. What is it that they are mindlessly scrolling past, and what does it say about the journey that they have been on? What is it that catches their attention, and how long do they hover over it for? What is on there that they like? What will they comment on?

It's a twist on a classic, but, rather than dropping breadcrumbs, these cookies will help your chosen one understand where they have been and potentially how far they have come on their journey. It might even be that something that they scroll past is the thing that finally propels them to put down their phone and carry on with their journey.

5

Accidental

Figure 5 *The heart of every story lies off the path, nowhere is this truer than with the accidental chosen one.*

The accidental storyline is playful, surprising, imaginative and often involves a level of magic or the supernatural. The absolute archetype here is *The Wizard of Oz* (1939), which hits every beat of the narrative arc, from the chosen one's arrival into the dark forest to their discovery that they always had the power to return home, if only they had looked deeply enough within themselves.

There are other widely accepted cinematic masterpieces that follow this paradigm, some of them involving no magic at all, one of the most famous of which is the 1988 Bruce Willis vehicle *Die Hard*, in which embittered New York cop John McClane finds himself transported, through no fault of his own, into a firestorm of guns and explosions in the heart of Los Angeles, when all he really wants to do is have a quiet Christmas attempting to make amends with his estranged wife, Holly.

While *Back to the Future* (1985), *Gravity* (2013) and *Big* (1988) all successfully thrust their chosen ones into unexpected and alien worlds where they are all left with one overwhelming desire – to go home – it is the Hitchock classic, *North by Northwest* (1959) that most closely apes *The Wizard of Oz*'s success in building a satisfying and progressively more interesting narrative, from innocent advertising man Roger Thornhill being mistaken for arch spy George Kaplan to the high-octane chase on Mount Rushmore.

It is worth pointing out here that Hitchock was a particular fan of the accidental storyline, employing it to great effect in many of his most successful films, including *The 39 Steps* (1935), in which the innocent Richard Hannay finds himself framed for murder; *Lifeboat* (1944), in which a group of survivors from a shipwreck are forced to share their boat with a German U-boat crewman; and *The Lady Vanishes* (1938), in which English tourist Iris Henderson finds herself embroiled in a web of deceit when she and her fellow train passengers are stranded in an isolated hotel.

What is at the heart of the accidental narrative?

The accidental storyline is identifiable by the methodology by which the chosen one enters the dark forest. If this is a sudden moment in which the chosen one has no element of choice, and if they are singularly ill-equipped to deal with this alien world into which they have been thrust, then you have an accidental narrative on your hands.

If your accidental chosen one asks themselves the question, 'Who am I?', at the beginning of this story, they will answer that, in one way or another, they are a nobody. They have no particular reason to be in your story; they have no particular skills or personality traits that might find themselves of interest to you, the writer. They have, literally, no idea why they are there. Their narrative is all about their understanding of what home means to them.

At the point where our chosen one receives the invitation, they are violently and suddenly ripped from their once upon a time where they are comfortable and safe. They mourn their sudden and unexpected departure from this space, asking, 'Why am I here?' However, the question becomes a more reflective one as they reach the last throw of the dice, as they understand that their journey has profoundly changed how they feel about their once upon a time and their desire to return to it has only grown.

In the cli-fi feature *The End We Start From* (2023), a nameless woman is forced from her home by a severe weather event just as she gives birth to her first child. While on the road, she is constantly questioning herself in the hopes of finding the next safe place for her and the baby in her care. As we reach the last-throw-of-the-dice moment, she plays peekaboo with the child, asking it, 'Where am I?' The surface meaning of the line is evident, but the subtext of it is her processing the journey that she has been on to this point and an uncertainty of what comes next for them as they make the last push to return home to an uncertain future.

As with all of our story arcs, the accidental narrative requires a path, a gate, an adventure off the path, a wolf and a suit of armour, but it is the appearance of a gatekeeper in all successful versions of this narrative that make it unique and create the dynamic within the story that maintains the dramatic impetus from the entry into the dark forest to the return home. The gatekeeper in these stories negates the requirement for a key.

The gatekeeper: 'You shall not pass!'

There is often a clear path to an obvious gate in the accidental story. Just as Dorothy is sure that she will find a way home by arriving in the Emerald City and asking help from the Wizard, so John McClane needs to inform the authorities that the Nakatomi Plaza has been overrun by terrorists. That way, the plot will be foiled, and he will be able to enjoy his family Christmas. In *Back to the Future*, Marty McFly needs to source enough energy to power the DeLorean in order to propel himself and Doc Brown back to 1985. In *Gravity*, Dr Ryan Stone has to find a way to return to Earth following the catastrophic debris collision that has damaged her craft and the International Space Station. In *Big*, Josh Baskin must track down the Zoltar machine so that he can reverse his wish and return to his twelve-year-old life.

In *North by Northwest*, it takes some time for Roger Thornhill to realize where his dark forest is and why he is there, but the initial way out of his troubles is clear. Through a series of well-placed coincidences and accidents, Thornhill has been mistaken for George Kaplan, and he has been caught hovering over a dead body with the murder weapon in his hand. Hitchcock, with his first-class writer, Ernest Lehman, closes off all exit routes for Thornhill. The only route back to his once upon a time is if he finds the real George Kaplan … through the dark forest.

Whether your chosen one has entered a magical other-dimension or has found themselves in unfamiliar territory here on planet Earth, there must be only one potential exit for the accidental chosen one, and that is straight ahead, through the dark forest. Roger Thornhill's path is clear as he tracks Kaplan down, following clue after clue.

The path for each of our accidental chosen ones is relatively easy to achieve, depending on their skillset, but in each case, just as we, and the chosen one, thinks that they have achieved what they need to achieve in order to return home, a gatekeeper steps in and sends them back. They have more to do before they are allowed to finish their adventures. A strong gatekeeper is key to the writing of a successful accidental storyline, and the gatekeeper's refusal to allow the chosen one through the gate at their first attempt is inextricably tied up with that thing which the chosen one needs to understand in order to return home having learned their lesson.

In *Back to the Future*, Marty identifies the upcoming lightning strike as being their ticket home fairly early on. There is a set date on which he will be able to make his return; however, it is Marty's interactions off the path, before the lightning strike, that cause the problems that will force him to alter the past in order to reconcile the future. The young Doc Brown acts as an effective gatekeeper here when he informs Marty that he cannot return to the future until he has righted the wrongs he has wrought in his interactions with his mother-to-be. As Marty has eclipsed his father, George, in Lorraine's affections, he is forced to travel further and further off the path in order to secure his very existence. For a young man who has little regard for his parents at the beginning of the story, Marty's journey into the past and the intervention of the gatekeeper in upsetting his attempts to return to the future unscathed are the central elements from which he learns his parents' true worth and his own reliance upon them for his own happiness.

In *Gravity*, Dr Stone's revelations to Kowalski about her dead daughter form the basis for the lesson that she must learn before she is allowed to return home. As every element of her attempts to return home become progressively more and more difficult and she essentially gives up, or gives in to her grief, it is the return of Kowalski, just as Stone is preparing for death, that sets him up as the gatekeeper. Stone has decided that her only way home is through death, and she has accepted this, but Kowalski is able to show her another way. Despite her own deep sorrow and mourning for her daughter, he gets her to fight and to recognize that living is the answer. She metaphorically and literally sheds everything associated with her past on this final stage of the journey, emerging from the shuttle as it sinks to the bottom of the lake and shedding her spacesuit, which has been weighing her down throughout her journey.

In *Big*, unusually, it is Josh's friend, Billy, who pulls Josh towards the gate. Josh has been taken in by his life as a successful toy designer and his relationship with Susan, and he has all but forgotten that he wants to get home. Rather than the gatekeeper turning the chosen one away from the gate because they have yet to complete the task that will make them worthy of returning, in this case, the gatekeeper must remind the chosen one that the accidental world is not their world. In order to be truly happy, they must return home. This is a neat inversion of the role of the gatekeeper but still serves to teach the chosen one the important lesson they must learn in order to make the return.

Die Hard is as simple and direct as *The Wizard of Oz* in its construction. When John McClane finds himself transported to the strange world of the Nakatomi Plaza, he is initially as helpless as Dorothy in Oz. Yes, McClane is a hard-bitten New York cop, but, without a weapon or a pair of shoes he is very much the accidental chosen one desperate to get home from this unsought adventure. As we will discover, McClane even has his own Scarecrow and Cowardly Lion on this journey, but it is the gatekeeper that concerns us here. Just as the Wizard of Oz sets Dorothy off on the task of stealing the Wicked Witch of the West's broomstick in order to return home, so McClane all but completes his mission to save the hostages at the Nakatomi Plaza when he alerts beat Sergeant Al Powell of the terrorist attack on the building. The arrival of the FBI and the cutting off of the power to the building, however, which under normal circumstances should end the siege, only creates more problems for McClane. Hans Gruber acts as gatekeeper for McClane, sending him back into the fray just as he thinks that all is done. Only by eventually making the journey personal, by involving his wife Holly, will McClane be able to make the return to his once upon a time.

For Roger Thornhill, his discovery that George Kaplan doesn't exist effectively closes the gate on him, but there is also a clear gatekeeper in the appearance of Eve Kendall who will be instrumental in showing Thornhill not only how to exit the dark forest but also how to improve his life following his return to his once upon a time.

The path: The Yellow Brick Road

Despite the fact that the gate is identifiable from the earliest stages of the narrative, the route down the path is not necessarily an easy one. After all, even Dorothy fell asleep in a poppy field on the way to the Emerald City. It is, however, the journey off the path that provides the real story here. Often this journey occurs after the chosen one has reached the gate only to be turned away, or, as in the case of *Back to the Future* and *Big*, when the chosen one's return is placed beyond them for a period of time during which they must interact with the accidental world and, inadvertently, become their own wolf.

For the chosen one who reaches the gate only to be turned back, the journey to the gate is relatively short. We are only two-thirds of the way through *The Wizard of Oz* when the Wizard sets Dorothy off on her quest to steal the Wicked Witch of the West's broomstick. John McClane dumps the body of the dead terrorist on Powell's car, and Stone reaches the International Space Station at around halfway through their respective screenplays.

The brilliance of *North by Northwest*, as with *The Wizard of Oz*, is in the layering up of the dangers and obstacles facing the chosen one as they progress through the dark forest. Each of these narratives provides a masterclass for any of us attempting to write one of these narratives. This is one of the reasons why the gatekeeper is so important. You should be concocting a storyline that is as surprising to your audience as it is to your chosen one, and the presence of the gate early on helps with the simplicity of the storytelling. You are making it absolutely clear what your chosen one must achieve before not allowing them to exit until they have explored the dark forest further. It is the gatekeeper's greater understanding of the nature of the gate and how to pass through it that makes this character so essential to the narrative. The chosen one has fallen into this world without any forethought and without any clear understanding of why they are here. The gatekeeper provides them with the necessary clues to finding their journey home. In *North by Northwest*, Eve Kendall knows that George Kaplan doesn't exist, and she is aware of the greater danger Phillip Vandamm poses which must be tackled before Thornhill will be allowed to leave the dark forest.

To return to the archetypal accidental narrative briefly, when Dorothy treads the path towards the Emerald City, it is here that she picks up her travel companions: the Scarecrow, the Tin Man and the Cowardly Lion. While accidental chosen ones do not always gather friends, supporters or characters who need help along the way, these can be a useful element to the path that will enable your chosen one more easily to navigate the section of the screenplay off the path following the intervention of the gatekeeper. Dorothy's companions clearly represent different aspects of her own personality, which she needs to recognize and overcome in order to return home, but there are interesting ways in which they can manifest themselves in these narratives. For John McClane, his driver Argyle and the underdog cop Powell are his own Scarecrow and Cowardly Lion. Argyle is a happy-go-lucky limo driver whose only role early on in the film is to be super-helpful and offer to wait out McClane's hopeful reunion with his estranged wife. By creating a small personal connection early on, Argyle is well positioned to be instrumental in overcoming Gruber's gang, just as the Scarecrow is instrumental in overcoming the Wicked Witch of the West. Equally, Powell is introduced as a cop who's lost his edge and become buried in bureaucracy, but it will take his interactions with McClane to identify a kindred spirit and help him to regain his own credibility and belief in himself, just as the Cowardly Lion comes to realize he is no coward after all.

Companions in *Big* and *Back to the Future* are companions of the heart whose job it is to divert Josh and Marty from the gate, but they are of equal use and importance in building complexity into the storytelling and adding richness and depth to the heart of the scripts. These companion figures, doubling up as gatekeepers, also allow the chosen one insight into their own characters and journeys home.

Gravity uses the idea of the companion somewhat differently in that Stone and Kowalski are bound to one another from the start, but it is Kowalski's self-sacrifice and his ability to 'return' to Stone at her greatest hour of need that make him into such a pivotal figure in the centre of the narrative. Stone loses Kowalski just as she reaches the end of the path and arrives at the gate, and her journey off the path is largely solitary, but Kowalski's presence as companion/gatekeeper affects many aspects of this story. Kowalski is, essentially, two different characters here: the brave leader who sacrifices himself for Stone and the companion with psychological insight who enables her to summon her last ounces of strength to make the final return home. Eve, in *North by Northwest*, becomes more than just a companion for Thornhill. She becomes the key that will help him to exit the dark forest.

In *Furiosa: A Mad Max Saga* (2024), we see the young Furiosa brutally snatched from her once upon a time: the idyllic oasis that is the Green Place of Many Mothers. Her initial and most powerful motivation (which is slightly complicated as the narrative progresses) is to return to her home. The arm on which she tattoos the path that she will take to return becomes a clear motif of her desire to do just this. However, out of necessity and her powerful will to survive, she literally tears this from her body in order to escape certain death at the hands of Dementus. After returning to the Citadel, she replaces her arm with a weapon of war, signalling to the audience that her path has now altered as she lusts for revenge against the man who has taken everything from her. The pull to her home still remains strong though, and you sense that maybe one day, after the sequel, she will find her way back.

As you develop your accidental storyline, consider this section of the script as being the prelude to the real struggle to come. The path will set your chosen one up for the trials ahead, and you may well find that including companions with a specific role to play in your chosen one's journey home will help you to create a dynamic set of sequences as your chosen one heads off the path. Even if you decide not to make use of companions, you are going to need a gatekeeper whose sole job it is to stop your chosen one from exiting through the gate and sending them back deep into the dark forest and off the path.

Off the path: 'Why am I here?'

Aided by the intervention of the gatekeeper generally at a point somewhere between the mid-point of the script and the end of the third act, your chosen one will be forced off the path because, to all intents and purposes, the path no longer exists. What began, for our chosen ones, as a journey with a clear goal and clear endpoint has become complicated by the short trip to the gate which has revealed to them the truth: that they must dig deep if they are going to discover the key which will allow them to open the gate and return home.

The key

There is no key.

Off the path (again): 'I'm still here!'

As in all of our paradigms, the journey off the path is the most dramatically satisfying section of your chosen one's journey. All chosen ones will travel off the path for different reasons. In the case of the accidental chosen one, the reason is that they have exhausted the path and have been blocked from exiting the dark forest through the gate. They have been sent to complete a task by the gatekeeper either explicitly or because the chosen one recognizes that they have no alternative. Just as the Wizard of Oz sets Dorothy off on a side quest to steal the Wicked Witch of the West's broomstick, so John McClane's focus shifts from alerting the authorities to the presence of Gruber and his gang to saving the lives of the hostages virtually single-handed and, specifically, the life of his estranged wife, Holly. In both cases, the completion of this task will lead to the discovery of that thing which will release the chosen one from the story.

North by Northwest is a story that is particularly effective and chimes so deeply and emotionally because the thing that will release Thornhill from the dark forest is also the gatekeeper and is also the thing which will change him deeply as a character: Eve Kendall. Eve plays a number of pivotal roles in this story, helping with the simplicity of a quite convoluted tale, and certainly helping to provide a satisfying emotional ending for Thornhill as the external spy ring is foiled but also his internal conflicted nature is healed through his relationship with Eve.

The point with the accidental storyline is that the chosen one is going to be allowed to exit the dark forest through their own rite of passage. They must confound the gatekeeper's plans to discover the truth: that they had the power to return home all along if only they had recognized the power of the ruby slippers on their feet. The gatekeeper is essentially duplicitous in their attempts to keep the chosen one within the dark forest. This duplicity may be deliberate and underhanded, or it may, in itself, be accidental or unintentional.

In *Back to the Future*, Lorraine has no idea that Marty is her son. Marty interacts with her almost immediately upon his arrival in the past. The path has already been diverted from even before it has established itself. At the midpoint of the film, when the young Doc Brown tells Marty that interacting with the past could have serious repercussions on future events, the repercussions have already begun. Marty's clear route to the gate at Doc Brown's house is now not so clear. Doc Brown sends Marty deep into the dark forest to rectify the mistakes he has made in interacting with Lorraine. The journey off the path, therefore, is unpredictable, fraught with mortal danger, both deadly serious and highly comic, establishing *Back to the Future* as one of the finest and most imaginative comedies of the 1980s.

After the disaster at the International Space Station, Stone's journey in *Gravity* is decidedly off the path. From the fire at the space station to the tangled cables and the lack of power in the Soyuz capsule, this is a relentless journey for survival against all odds. This journey is so far off any charted path that we engage with Stone's attempts to realign herself with the fast-disappearing gate with our hands to our mouths. As with all accidental narratives, though, there is a lesson that Stone needs to learn before she can pass through the gate which will allow her to return home. Just as Marty McFly needs to recognize that his parents have value in his life and he learns to respect them, so Stone has to recognize the value of life. She lost her child, and she still mourns for that loss. The vision she has of Kowalski in the latter stages of the film leads her to understand that she values life and, specifically her own life. Kowalski is, of course, Stone's individual vision here so whatever he says to her is actually her speaking to herself, just as the Tin Man, Scarecrow and Cowardly Lion represent aspects of Dorothy's own personality. When Kowalski says, 'You gotta plant both feet on the ground and start livin' life', that is her message to herself. She has learned her lesson, and the last, harrowing sequence of the film can begin.

As we have seen, *Big* works in a similar way to *Back to the Future* in that Josh is distracted from the gate by events in the accidental dark forest that move him away from the gate. There is a difference here in that Marty McFly inadvertently sets off a chain of events which he must rectify in order to make his return, while Josh Baskin is enticed by the world that he inhabits as an adult. Josh does not have a Doc Brown gatekeeper ordering him to return to the dark forest to create the right conditions for his return. Instead, the gatekeeper here is time itself. It will take six weeks for Josh to be able to access the Zoltar machine, and, in those six weeks, he must spend time off the path. He has no choice but to spend his time as an adult off the path, and it is the life he leads there that is so enticing to him. A different telling of this story would see Josh as a mistaken/accidental chosen one, and he would never leave his adult world, preferring the life of independence, money, success and a real girlfriend to that of a twelve-year-old boy. *Big*, however, is a feel-good family comedy, and, as such, Josh must learn something about himself on his journey and realize that this is not the world he belongs in. Unlike most accidental scenarios, Josh enjoys his time a little too much in his accidental world but ultimately realizes that the world of adulthood is a world of responsibilities and routines, whereas the freedom of childhood is something to be cherished, a freedom he didn't recognize when his mother was telling him to take out the trash and do his homework.

The key, then, in the accidental narrative, is replaced by a gatekeeper who points the chosen one towards a greater understanding of themselves. Only by overcoming their past traumas, their hang-ups, their misconceptions or their character flaws will they be able to bypass the gatekeeper and return to their once upon a time.

The wolf: Do we need a wolf?

For most of our accidental chosen ones, the dark forest is a frightening enough place without requiring a wolf as well. However, wolves do appear in these narratives but often in different forms to those found on other dramatic pathways. While Hans Gruber, for instance, is clearly a wolf, in *Die Hard* the wolf and the dark forest are inextricable from one another. The wolf is the dark forest. He created it and he runs it, in much the same way as the Wicked Witch of the West is the personification of that which makes Oz so alien and frightening to Dorothy. Trapped by the witch, this is the point at which Dorothy calls out directly to Aunt Em begging to return. Gruber literally brings McClane's family into the story when his children appear on television and Gruber recognizes Holly as McClane's wife. This moment brings all of McClane's desires to a head. Just as the witch holds Dorothy a prisoner as far away from Aunt Em as it is possible for her to be, so Gruber holds all of the power in making Holly as inaccessible to McClane as it is possible to be. The role of the wolf here, then, is the same: to have the chosen one recognize what it is that is most important to them so that they will fight all the harder and dig all the deeper in order to achieve it.

Back to the Future has a rather mild wolf in the form of Biff, but he is more of a complicating factor in Marty's story than a specific antagonist to Marty. Biff inadvertently threatens Marty's existence rather than overtly setting out to destroy him. The dark forest and all that happens therein is really Marty's antagonist here. The series of events begun when Marty discovered George in the tree proliferate, and Biff is just an element in that proliferation. There is no real, single wolf in *Back to the Future* except Marty himself.

Similarly, *Gravity* and *Big* have no overt wolves that threaten our chosen ones. The wolves are, once again, the dark forest itself and, just as importantly, our central characters' coming to terms with themselves, their pasts and their futures. *Gravity* is a film about loss; *Big* is a film about childhood. In both cases, those themes loom large over the storylines and are representative of the antagonism within, which is in direct conflict with the outward action of the film. Stone almost gives in to the relentless forces mitigating against her return to Earth because of the loss she feels for her dead child. Josh almost decides to remain as an adult because he has forgotten the importance and carefree values of his own childhood and all that that entails.

Vandamm, the wolf in *North by Northwest*, in keeping with other wolves, if they exist, on the accidental pathway is inextricably linked with the dark forest. Vandamm and these other wolves created the dark forest, and the dark forest can only be left if they are defeated. The real, emotional journey of the accidental chosen one, however, is an internal one. Their journey from the innocent, naive character who stumbles into this alien world to the capable, triumphant hero who leaves it will form the answers to the question 'Why am I here?' posed at the beginning and end of the narrative journey.

The chosen one must overtly recognize and overcome their conflicted natures if they are to return to their once upon a time and, by specifically identifying what it is that is keeping your chosen one in their accidental world, you will be able to fashion a wolf or a force that acts as a wolf which will be keeping them a prisoner until such time as they recognize it as such.

The suit of armour: It's holding you back …

Typically, our accidental chosen one enters their adventure with no recognisable suit of armour. John McClane even divests himself of his shoes, making him still more vulnerable to the dangers that lie ahead. Everything about this accidental world must be made as far out of our chosen one's comfort zones as possible. Marty McFly looks out of place in the 1950s wearing his 1980s gear, made clear when he is asked why he's wearing a life preserver. He is quite literally an alien in this world, a joke that is picked up a little later in the narrative in a night-time confrontation with George. The very trappings of the capable astronaut are shed by Stone as she, step by step, moves through the story of *Gravity*. As writer-director Alfonso Cuarón made clear, 'She's trapped in her spacesuit.' The very armour which is designed to keep her safe is not enough in this frightening situation. In *Big*, Josh must adopt the trappings of an adult in order to while away his time before he and Billy can track down the Zoltar machine. These clothes are not made for him and do not suit him, and he must remove them if he is ever to decide to return to his once upon a time.

Sometimes, in these storylines, the chosen one carries with them a talisman or seemingly innocuous item which will turn out to have great meaning for them as they reach the conclusion of the narrative. Dorothy, of course, has her ruby slippers, but others, too, hold something close which will be the secret or an element of the secret that enables them to return home. While one of the strengths of *Die Hard* is that McClane fights back with nothing, his aim and escape route are much clearer than others on this pathway. Marty McFly has the family photograph in which he sees himself being gradually erased from existence, and Stone carries with her the memory of her child, brought to touching life by the sound of the crying baby on the radio in the closing stages of the film. Unusually for the accidental story arc, Josh Baskin has an actual person, in the shape of Billy, to pull him back to reality when he most needs it. In the absence of a suit of armour, our accidental chosen ones cling, instead, onto icons or talismans that will bring them, eventually, back to their once upon a time.

It is Eve Kendall who provides the suit of armour for Roger Thornhill in *North by Northwest*. Just as Dorothy relies on her friends in her time of greatest need, so Thornhill's growing relationship with Eve provides him with the armour he needs to negotiate the final stages of the story. In another form, this film would be a romantic comedy, throwing two mismatched characters into a situation where they are forced to interact, but *North by Northwest* is so much more than this by placing these characters within an accidental storyline. The female character, here, is stronger than the male. She provides him with the means to exit the gate. This film is not, as a romantic comedy is, a meeting of equals. Eve is Thornhill's superior in almost every way, and the journey Thornhill takes is one of studied independence to shared love. His independence is the suit of armour he sheds by the end of the film.

Asking themselves, 'Why am I here?', as they exit the dark forest, the answer will be very different for these chosen ones. Through the unexpected intervention of an unasked-for narrative, they have discovered something about themselves that they did not previously know. The answer may now be, 'I am a better person', or 'I am worthy of love', or 'I finally love myself.' Whatever the answer, it is a direct answer to the confusion of their answer in the first act of your screenplay.

The accidental narrative can be used in a host of different scenarios and genres and provides rich material and possibilities for characters lost and out of their depth in unfamiliar landscapes. Using and manipulating the tools outlined above, you can fashion a surprising and original piece while maintaining drama throughout and keeping focus on the main thrust of the narrative: the chosen one's inner journey to the enlightenment that will allow them to sidestep the gatekeeper, pass through the gate and return to their once upon a time.

Exercises

One (wo)man show

It's a daunting thing getting up on stage and holding everyone's attention as you monologue at them for over an hour. However, once your accidental chosen one returns home, not only will they have the courage to do just that, but they will also have an amazing story to tell that will no doubt be gripping for an audience to hear. As part of this exercise, have your accidental chosen one head up to the Edinburgh Fringe with nothing but their pre-prepared script and a pocket full of dreams. What are the most entertaining parts of their adventure that they would open with? When was it that they thought they might have jacked it all in and called it a day? How did they come to the realisation that they had to see this thing through and finally, after arriving home how do they showcase the new appreciation that they have for this space?

If you are looking for inspiration for this activity, take a look at *Baby Reindeer* (2024) and *Fleabag* (2016) which showcase chosen ones who did just that. Furthermore, although we will only be touching lightly on the subject of TV in this book, it could be argued that both of them are, in fact, accidental chosen ones.

Up in the attic

Your chosen one who is involved in an accidental narrative has a powerful and emotive connection to the home from which they have been taken. What would happen if they were presented with a box of all of their old stuff that someone has found in their attic? What would be in there? What emotions would it evoke within them? How are the things in the box representative of the attachment(s) that they have to the place or people that are there? It might be good to think about where your chosen one is in their narrative journey when they receive this box as it will assist you in developing the physical, emotional, psychological or spiritual response that they have to what they find there.

Title sequence

Title sequences for films are a thing of beauty all on their own. From Saul Bass's incredible openings for Hitchcock's films to the various times when Bond comes to shoot out at an audience framed in a gun barrel before red slowly drips down the screen, they settle an audience into the narrative they are about to see.

Think about the images and imagery that you would want to see in your opening title sequence and create a mood board of this. To further the exercise, you might want to construct a timed PowerPoint to the music you think would fit the piece or potentially jump into an editing software you feel comfortable using and creating your titles on there. If you are feeling confident with this, it is also good to start thinking about who you might want to direct and star in the piece you are writing and place their names in the credit sequence. It gives a clear indication of the tone you are wanting to showcase in your work and begins to expand your industry knowledge. As an aside, Christopher Nolan or Sofia Coppola are going to be a little busy so might not be available. Try and look for emerging talent in the genre that you are writing. They are much more likely to be looking for great work to attach themselves to.

6

Mistaken

Figure 6 *The most terrifying of wolves stalk our mistaken chosen ones … or they end up becoming one.*

Not everyone can be a chosen one. In order for the best of us to be able to showcase their special status in the world, there has to be an equal and opposite end of the scale for those of us who may want to plumb the depths of depravity, chaos and horror. These chosen ones, unlike their altruistic cousins, are here to tell us tales of woe and warning. They are on a subversion of the other four pathways on offer for us writers. After being invited into a dark forest there is little chance of them ever emerging, and, depending on the type of narrative you are telling, it is either that they regret ever starting this adventure or revel in the darkness that they find in the sordid corners of the space they now have to call home whether they like it or not.

Your mistaken chosen one must perform an action mistakenly or without total thought as to the ramifications during their invitation sequence. They will now have to spend the remainder of the piece trying to deal with that mistake, often only making things worse. It may be that they have signed a bum deal that they are now unable to get out of, like mistaken/unknowing chosen one Tyler does in *The Menu* (2022). The match that they strike doesn't burn down the dark forest but rather torches their once upon a time (and usually themselves), as Thelonious 'Monk' Ellison ends up doing in the mistaken/willing narrative *American Fiction* (2023) in a rather meta finale. There's the chance that after accidentally falling down a rabbit hole there is no way back to a home they are desperately searching for as it is for mistaken/accidental chosen ones Rose in *Smile* (2022) or Brynn in *No One Will Save You* (2023). It could happen that the mentor they are hoping will arrive never does, or, if they do, the chosen one will actively ignore the wisdom they are trying to bestow, or the mentor will actually encourage them to allow the darkness that they have inside them to come out. Mistaken/unable-to-believe chosen one Owen in *I Saw the TV Glow* (2024) is never fully able to follow his mentor Maddy on the path she sets out for him and is then trapped in a dark forest where he is never able to showcase that he is a swan inside. With all of these chosen ones, as they begin to further explore the dark forest, they realize that the journey they thought they were on is not actually going to present them with the answers they first thought it would. Instead, they will now become lost in a dark forest of their own creation or take on in earnest the mantle of the wolf.

A classic narrative worth engaging with to clearly illustrate this paradigm in full is the Billy Wilder classic *Sunset Boulevard* (1950) where screenwriter Joe Gillis agrees to write a script for an ageing starlet who draws him into a terrifying dark forest from which there is no escape. The image of Gillis floating face down in a swimming pool during the prologue is one of the more iconic in film history and immediately gives us a clear indication as to the tone and thematic content of the piece. The results of his initial deal cannot be undone because he entered into the contract in bad faith. Also, the starlet, Norma Desmond, with whom he made his deal, is unstable and unpredictable.

A more modern interpretation of this subversion of the paradigm would be the South Korean film *Decision to Leave* (2022) where detective Jang Hae-jun mistakenly falls in love with Song Seo-rae, a suspect in a murder case he is investigating. This 'deal' he unfortunately makes has a vast array of unintended consequences for him that will trap him (and her) in a dark forest of his/their own creation.

There is also the Japanese horror classic *Ring* (1998), which helped cultivate a subgenre in the West known as J-horror. In the narrative, journalist Reiko

Asakawa mistakenly watches a cursed videotape, which means she has seven days until she dies. However, it turns out that if she can make a copy of the tape and show it to someone else, she can survive but at the expense of another victim. She will be able to return home but must forever live with the ramifications of her actions. This type of slow-burn procedural element of a narrative can be seen as a clear road map for similar titles such as *It Follows* (2014), *Smile*, *The Autopsy of Jane Doe* (2016) and even *Longlegs* (2024), wherein our chosen one mistakenly awakens a curse that they have no chance of running from. These chosen ones are swept up by a force entirely outside of their control which they have little to no hope of taming, and even if they do it never feels like the success that those on the positive paradigms are able to enjoy.

When penning a story along these lines, always be thinking, *It can't get any worse than this, can it?* Then make sure that it does … at least for your chosen one. The audience will thank you for it … or end up watching through the gaps in their fingers.

What is at the heart of the mistaken narrative?

At the centre of any mistaken paradigm is the initial 'sin' that our chosen one commits. Ultimately, that is the thing that best represents their conflicted nature. At their core, they are either unwise, impulsive and misguided, or bitter, resentful and angry. These traits cause them to respond to an invitation that they should really have avoided, but now that they have made the unwise decision, they must watch the fallout happen around them. Their sin is the thing that becomes them as they slowly succumb to it and they allow it to fully infect them.

Within these narratives, the question of, 'Who am I?', now morphs into, 'What have I done?', This question is inextricably linked to the central sin of the piece. Initially, the mistaken chosen one believes that their response to the invitation is something that they might be able to live with. They have only killed the goose. The mistake that they have made will soon be forgotten and might even make for an interesting story later down the line. However, as they journey through the dark forest, they soon come to learn that this initial decision has trapped them within this new space, and they now must pay for their sin(s).

In the Icelandic horror *Lamb* (2021), a husband and wife take care of a sheep–human hybrid child as their own and kill the mother who birthed it. In making this choice, they have disrupted the natural order of the world, and, come the last throw of the dice, realize that their selfish actions have consequences when the father to the child (a ram/man hybrid) comes looking for revenge. The 'What have I done?' of this narrative has haunted them from the first time they have asked this question of themselves and have entirely unravelled their lives.

The Menu and *No One Will Save You* are about chosen ones who are individual sinners. Brynn, in *No One Will Save You*, has been shunned by her community after the terrible thing that she did to her childhood best friend, Maude. Tyler, in *The Menu*, has agreed to be one of the diners as part of chef Julian Slowik's theatrical last meal despite knowing the ramifications of accepting the invitation. However, he doesn't know that Julian intends to further humiliate him in front of the rest of his staff. This is the part of the deal that he doesn't understand when he is in the process of accepting his opportunity to dine at the exclusive restaurant.

Both *American Fiction* and *Smile* deal with much broader societal sins. Although both our chosen ones in these narratives have flaws that are obvious to the audience, the films become vehicles to develop stories about the thematic ideas at the heart of the arc our chosen ones are on. Although Thelonious, in *American Fiction*, only constructs a false identity for the book *My Pafology* to mock the literary establishment for their obsession with stereotypes expected from Black writers, when he learns of the money he will make from a book deal, he is soon won round. The piece is clearly exploring the treatment of race in modern-day America and the performative nature of the culture industry when dealing with complicated questions around identity. *Smile* not only nakedly leans into the genre conceits of horror but also still manages to tell a story of how trauma is passed between individuals.

Finally, there are the familial sins where our chosen one responds to the invitation as a result of the sins that have been passed down through their bloodline. Remaining true to the biblical definition, this is the sins of one generation being passed onto the next. *Talk to Me* (2022), *The Godfather*

(1972) and *Longlegs* are clear examples of this. In *The Godfather*, Michael Corleone starts the narrative as a fair and just man; however, he is sucked into a life of criminality when there is an attempt made on his father's life and he has to take over the family 'business'. In *Talk to Me*, Mia's obsession with the suicide of her mother is the thing that leads her to further experiment with the embalmed hand that allows her to see dead people which eventually drives her to madness and her death. *Longlegs* has FBI agent Lee Harker uncover that the titular psychotic killer has a personal connection to her mother and the sins that she has committed to save her daughter from the murderous dolls that he creates.

There is often an inherent irony wrapped up within the narrative of a mistaken arc: that our chosen one frequently believes they are on one pathway when in fact, as the writer (and the audience) know, they are not working towards a happily ever after but will in fact end up lost within the dark forest. This clear subversion is important and must always be at the back of your mind should you be writing a mistaken arc. How and when your chosen one realizes that they are truly lost as they approach the gate during their journey can be a powerful dramaturgical tool for you as a writer. Too soon and we are denied the tension of the build-up; too late and we are not able to squirm in our seats as our chosen one attempts one last time to escape. While there are four clear versions of the mistaken narrative, and the possibilities for reinvention and subversion of these stories is almost limitless, you will still have to consider how your chosen one will answer the question, 'What have I done?', at the opening of your story. The likelihood is that, for most of our mistaken chosen ones, they will respond with a lie. They are the heroes of their own stories, but their stories are twisted and warped. They may well see themselves as righteous, heroic or entrepreneurial, but we will be able to see them as they really are: self-serving.

The wolf: 'What big teeth you have'

We start with the wolf in this paradigm because of the importance they have to your mistaken screenplay. They are often the reason the audience has come to watch your film in the first place. For a mistaken narrative, you will need to consider very carefully how you render this particular element of your story. An effective or ineffective wolf will make or break the story that you are wanting to tell.

There is an old adage in horror that the lesser the monster the lesser the movie. More often than not it isn't the homogenous sets of teenagers that we flock to the cinema to see chopped into pieces but rather the mad axe-wielding men and women who chase them down and facilitate their demise. *The Texas Chain Saw Massacre* (1974) is nothing without Leatherface, just as much as there is no *Friday the 13th* (1980) without Jason. In these slasher versions of the narrative that we would recognize as an accidental/mistaken paradigm, these wolves are the literal embodiments of everything that our chosen one fears the most. They are a literal manifestation of the sin that plagues them and mean that as a writer you can have them confront a physical version of what may be an incorporeal thing. They are the predators that hunt for the prey of our chosen ones.

In *Decision to Leave*, Song Seo-rae represents excitement and an escape from the drudgery of our chosen one's everyday life. However, in his lust for her, he allows her to destroy vital evidence, gaslight him and ultimately kill again. With *Smile*, Rose's trauma is expressed in the terrifying smirk that the monster presents to the world through those that it has possessed.

There are also the versions of these arcs where our chosen ones slowly but surely transform into the wolf. Any goodness that may or may not have been within them when we first met them within their once upon a time is washed away as they begin to realize that they can become the wolf of this dark forest, and it allows them to finally become the truest version of themselves and truthfully answer that all-important question, 'What have I done?'

They might also usurp the current wolf who stalks the forest only to become a greater terror than they could have first imagined. In *The Godfather*, Micheal slowly begins to realize that not only is he adept at running his family's criminal enterprise but that he might also enjoy the power and the status that it affords him. He allows his worlds to collapse into one and begins to see himself as crime lord first and family man second, culminating in him shutting the door on his wife as the first film ends, thereby betraying the promise that he made to her at the beginning of the piece.

Brynn, in *No One Will Save You*, manages to outwit the alien invaders to the point where she is able to live among them in a paradise that is seemingly of her own creation where she is able to dance in the street as she wanted to at the beginning without having to fully confront her sins – a far cry from the world of her once upon a time where she was spat at and subjected to abusive phone calls.

The path: It's getting dark

Initially, the path starts off as clear as it would be for the other paradigms that you might be writing. It is the element that not only allows for the narrative trajectory of the piece but also ensures that you are able to play with the ironic interplay between audience and chosen one. The chosen one has less of an understanding of the journey that they are actually on than the audience.

In *Ring*, Asakawa believes that, by solving the curse, she will be free of the malevolent Sadako. She thinks that she is an accidental chosen one who must simply return home with a renewed appreciation for her family. Joe Gillis, in *Sunset Boulevard*, truly thinks that the deal he has made is a good one, as do the Kim family in *Parasite* (2023). In Joe Gillis's eyes, he is an unknowing chosen one who will eventually be able to use this deal to his advantage. Initially, in *No One Will Save You*, Brynn believes that she will be able to stave off an entire alien invasion in her hometown where no one will speak to her. They all could not be more wrong in their estimation of the dark forest they are entering into, and their answers to the question 'What have I done?' will be very misguided.

You could write each one of these stories and have them as a traditional arc that has a happily ever after at the end; however, once you have committed to writing a mistaken story, you must clearly set out to an audience that this path will soon be absorbed into the dark forest and your chosen one will become lost and unable to find their way out.

Off the path: 'Can you help me? I'm lost'

During their journey into the dark forest, our chosen one will slowly begin to understand that their path is becoming increasingly hard to follow. How and when you allow this realization to come to our chosen one depends on the emotional journey you want to put them through and the subversion of the typical arc you are following. Often the midpoint of your narrative should contain the moment that our chosen one finally understands they are trapped and rapidly begins to make their situation worse as they either scramble to find another path that might take them to the exit or begin to hatch their diabolical plan to become the wolf.

Importantly, as the routes off the path and the path converge for our chosen one, we must see the terror or the bliss that they are experiencing. They are slowly being stretched on a medieval torture rack or a frog sitting in a pan of gradually boiling water. However, some of them actually like the experience, as it allows them to experience the pain and the pleasure of the status they believe they have always deserved.

As the narrative progresses and the routes on the path and off the path become one, our chosen ones can be divided into two camps: the panickers and the revellers. The panickers begin to realize that this is happening and there is no way out of the mess they have got themselves into. They gradually begin to understand that they have no control over the decision they made in the opening of the piece and are slowly finding that they are unable to undo the harm they have done by responding to it. However, it is during this realization that our revellers start to understand how they might be able to take advantage of this unravelling situation for their own nefarious ends.

This is also the space in our mistaken one's dark forest where they finally understand the central sin that they are in the process of exploring as part of the thematic arc of the piece.

In *Ring*, Asakawa realizes that the curse from the videotape is too strong. Even after coming to terms with her conflicted nature and attempting to appease the spirit of the dead Sadako that she finds at the bottom of the well, nothing she tries will stop her. It also allows her to come to terms with her own 'poor parenting' of her son Yōichi and how she has to strive to be a 'better mother'. Hers is a sin of neglect; however, there is such a great weight of Japanese cultural and societal expectations hanging over this issue that this seemingly fairly innocuous sin doesn't necessarily fully translate to a Western audience.

Decision to Leave has one of the more overt nods to the total collapse of the path and off the path. As Jang Hae-jun allows his infatuation for Song Seo-rae to continue to cloud his judgement, the case he is working on slips further and further out of his grasp. This continues until the closing act where he desperately searches for Song Seo-rae on a beach with little to no hope of finding her as she has been entirely consumed by the dark forest as a result of the decisions they have made together. His is a forest entirely constructed from his lust and unfaithfulness to his wife and his profession.

In *Late Night with the Devil* (2023), Jack Delroy has his path set out clearly where he will mistakenly exploit the young Lilly, who is possessed, on live TV in order to save his show and his career. However, as this response to his invitation begins to unfold and he loses control of the demonic creature that is a part of her, his world collapses in and he has to confront the painful truth of his dead wife and the part he may have played in her demise. His is the sin of greed that left him dissatisfied with the life that he had, always chasing the next goal at the expense of those around him.

With *American Fiction*, the lie that Monk has told to gain his lucrative publishing deal overtakes his life. He lashes out at those who he loves who actually liked the book that he first wrote and ends up sabotaging the relationship that he has with Coraline because of it. He is unable to see through the dark forest that he has created around him because of his initial sin of pride.

This notion of a sin committed and a subsequent price to pay will help you to keep to the formula of *Simple story, complex character* as you develop your storyline. All of these sins are simple and communicable in no more than a word or two, but the guilt that lives within the chosen one forms the basis of a deeply conflicted, fascinating central character.

Suit of armour: A paddle in the shallows

With the two distinct versions of the chosen ones that are typically found within these dark forests, it stands to reason that they come into them wearing very different suits of armour. Bear with us here … You'll notice the aquatic theme running through this element and the next (the gate) that will hopefully make even more sense when you have read both segments.

For those who come to regret that they ever responded to the invitation in the first place, they come wearing a swimsuit. It is more than likely that they look good in whatever it is that they are wearing, and at the beginning of the narrative it is helping them to navigate this new world that they are traversing. In a slightly sadistic way, it gives them a thrill to be so exposed to danger at the start and allows them to explore the more exhilarating and novel elements of the dark forest. However, as the world begins to darken, and the path and off the path begin to converge, they start to understand the impracticalities of what they have on and how they are actually rather exposed to the elements. As they continue to see control slip away from them, they will bemoan their lack of foresight in not being more prepared for this adventure, or they will have to sacrifice much more than they intended to when they first entered into the dark forest. These narratives have a wolf that stalks the dark forest that is so powerful that there is no defeating them no matter what actions our chosen one takes.

With Joe in *Sunset Boulevard*, the irony of his final resting place being floating face down in a pool is delicious. He believed that he had a handle on the deal that he made at the beginning of the piece; however, it begins to very quickly spiral away from him, and it appears that he is not at all ready or willing to do the things that he needs to do in order to fully see the deal through.

In *The Menu*, Tyler is initially more than happy with everything at Slowik's restaurant and even understands that his very life is at risk if he continues to dine at the establishment. He believes that he has full control of the situation that he is in and has a full understanding of what makes for a culinary experience. However, when challenged to cook a meal in the kitchen as part of the menu, Tyler is exposed as a fraud as he is unable to deliver. The gap in his knowledge is showcased to everyone, and he is left exposed and demeaned. He is a fraud, and behind his ego there is no substance.

Rose, in *Smile*, suffers a similar fate in that she is facing up against another force that she has no hope of defeating. At the beginning of the narrative, she believes that she will be able to break the curse that is hanging over her. As she digs into the past that haunts her, however, she discovers that even despite her professional training as a therapist she is unable to defeat the evil that has hold of her. Instead, she has only made things worse as she has been navigating her dark forest that ultimately leads to her demise.

There are then those who revel in the darkness they find at the centre of the dark forest. These chosen ones are the ones that are destined to take on the mantle of the wolf at the centre of a dark forest that they are now able to call their own. At the start of these narratives, imagine that the chosen one is wearing a large metallic diving suit. It obviously makes it difficult for them to exist in their once upon a time; however, they are either unable or unwilling to take it off for reasons that are their own despite those around them telling them to remove it. As the narrative progresses, and the path and off the path bleed into one, they discover that they are much more able to move around as they have found a space they can readily navigate whilst keeping their armour on.

In *Thoroughbreds* (2017), the emotionally and psychologically damaged Amanda hatches a plan with her friend Lily to murder Lily's stepfather, Mark. Amanda proves remarkably adept at navigating this process and is able to not only attempt to arrange the killing but also to get the pair out of trouble when they overreach on occasion with drug dealer Tim, who they try to blackmail to carry out the murder. At the end of the piece, Amanda willingly consumes a drink that Lily has laced with Rohypnol so that Lily can murder her stepfather and blame it on Amanda. Having experienced the world in a dark forest of her creation, Amanda wishes to stay in it and be branded a murderer rather than return to her once upon a time where she doesn't fit in.

The gate: 'There's no way this will open'

Within this paradigm, there is no gate that our chosen ones are able to pass through. The only way they are able to escape from the dark forest is either through their death or, in the rare instance they escape death, by carrying the traumas they have experienced within it for the rest of their lives. The figure of the 'Final Girl' is the perfect representation of this idea.

For our mistaken chosen ones, when they reach the end of the dark forest, they realize that they are now faced with a large dam that is holding back a huge torrent of water. However, this dam is cracking under pressure, and, as the path and off the path become indistinguishable for our chosen one, more and more water is leaking out.

For our regretters in their swimming costumes, they don't mind this to begin with as they are initially dressed to get a little wet. However, as things become more serious, and a trickle turns to a torrent, they are unable to survive in such an environment. They finally realize that they are stuck in this dark forest that they have been trying to venture through and must accept that, in responding to the invitation at the beginning, this is the fate they deserve.

As Jack Delroy in *Late Night with the Devil* continually goads the demon out of the young Lily live on air, he becomes increasingly aware that although the ratings are great for the show, the consequences of his actions are becoming more and more dire. He was well prepared for some sensationalist, exploitative segments of his show but not a full confrontation with a malevolent otherworldly force.

Meanwhile, our revellers have seen their power grow and grow as the water rises around them. After all, they are equipped (either by design or mistake) not only to survive but to thrive in this space now that it is metaphorically flooded.

An effective modern example of this is *Saltburn* (2023), the story of an impoverished student at Oxford who tries to inveigle himself into the lives of the upper-class Catton family. Student Oliver Quick finds strength in being an outcast and an outsider in order to create the grift that will eventually see him unveil himself to the world (and us in the audience) as the wolf who has been stalking the dark forest this whole time. He has meticulously planned how he will ingratiate himself into the Catton family where he earns and exploits their trust. Nothing, it seems, is beyond Quick, and the further he embeds himself in his deceit, the further he is willing to go in order to reach his goal of finally taking Saltburn for himself.

The key: 'Where did I put that damned thing?'

As there is no gate, it goes without saying that there is no key. However, it doesn't mean that our chosen ones know this, and they might still be desperately searching for one in the hope that they might be able to escape. It might even be, if you are a particularly malevolent writer, that you might want to make it so that your chosen one believes that they might be able to leave the dark forest right up until their eventual demise only to cruelly keep them trapped and watch as they are finally subsumed into it.

Smile does this quite effectively as the narrative progresses through the middle third. Rose's reality begins to collapse with both her and the audience being constantly wrongfooted as to what is happening and what tricks her mind is playing on her. Meanwhile, in *American Fiction*, Monk has his journey summed up in the reflective conclusion of the piece with him deciding that his demise is the only way that the film can end. As a good writer, he has realized that there is no redemption for his character because he has lost himself in the dark forest that he has created.

Owen, in *I Saw the TV Glow*, is a regretter because he is lost among the thicket of his dark forest. Maddy offered him a terrifying opportunity to join her in a new life inside 'The Pink Opaque' that was the key to him escaping from his life of drudgery and oppression. However, he rejected this and will now be forever haunted by the possibilities that could have been.

Imagine these disparate chosen ones' answers to the question 'What have I done?' at this point in the narrative. Each of them will have come to a much clearer understanding of their sins. The mistaken story arc is much less about growing and changing than it is about looking deep within and realizing exactly who your characters are. The lies they told themselves at the beginnings of these narratives have been replaced by a brutal honesty.

Exercises

From the top rope!

The bombastic nature of wrestling is a great medium for character creation. Everything that takes place within the squared circle is elevated to an absurd degree. Both faces and heels have their constructed personas built, destroyed, reconstituted and restored across a physical melodramatic narrative that can last for years of sweat-drenched action.

In this exercise, we want you to reimagine your chosen one as the latest wrestling megastar that is going to enter the ring. Come up with their backstory, their costume, their walk-on music and their finishing move.

Always be placing character at the centre of the decisions you are making in this exercise. How is the work that you are doing here building a picture of the kind of personality that they have? Are they the face who will overcome the odds, fight fair and be the hero that we need, or are they the heel who fights dirty, always cheats and revels in the pantomime boos and jeers from the crowd?

Don't stop believin'

We all have a go-to karaoke song. With the right amount of social lubrication and peer pressure, even the most reluctant of us can be convinced to belt out that one tune we know well enough not to care that we can't hit the high note at the end.

However, what particular song is it that your chosen one would sing at karaoke? What is it that makes that song special to them? Do they actually enjoy karaoke, or have they been forced into attending? You might want to think about the individual lyrics that they stumble over, or the ones they can't even get out and why that is.

To expand the idea a little, it might be that they could make their next song a duet with the wolf that they are doing battle within the dark forest.

'We observe the monster in its natural habitat'

Write the script for a nature documentary about the wolf as it moves about your dark forest. It can be in any style that you want, but it's often fun to believe that the most famous nature documentarian in the world might be reading it aloud as part of his next special for the BBC. Really think about how this creature/person moves about the space that they are in. What special behaviours or traits could you observe that would make this particular segment an engaging watch for the audience at home? What is it that is unique/special about your wolf that would make for an interesting comment?

7

Willing case study
Inside Out 2 (2024)

Logline: When Anxiety arrives at Headquarters and starts causing chaos, Joy must rally the other emotions to make sure that Riley doesn't lose her sense of self.

Release Date: 14 June 2024

Screenwriters: Meg LeFauve, Dave Holstein, Kelsey Mann

Inside Out 2 is a great example of a creative allegory that works really effectively on screen. The first film in the franchise, *Inside Out* (2015), was created off the back of director Pete Docter's desire to better understand the psychological developments that were happening inside his young daughter as she began to grow older. This personal story continues into the sequel with Riley now experiencing the next big challenge of her life as she begins puberty and the range of changes she (and the emotions inside her head) will experience as she traverses this.

    Inside Out 2 is a brilliant watch for us writers as, throughout the narrative, Riley is constantly being offered choices that the emotions up in Headquarters then debate before deciding on the best course of action. Each of the emotions in turn have their own conflicted nature which is explicitly outlined in their character design. It is like seeing a character being constructed in real time while we are watching on.

    One of the most overt lessons that a writer can learn from watching *Inside Out 2* is how to construct a villain/wolf/antagonist. The antagonistic forces in Pixar films are not in the traditional vein of villainy. Typically, they will simply have the wrong answer to the central dramatic question rather than a nefarious plan to end the world as we know it. They will have built and/or own the dark forest through which the chosen one is journeying, but they have done so out of a desire to see their own ideological outlook succeed rather than to deliberately have others fail. Lots-o'-Huggin' in *Toy Story 3* (2010), who oversees Sunnyside Daycare like a dictator of his own banana republic, does so because of his feelings of abandonment that he experienced when he was replaced by his child, Daisy. Anton Ego, the harsh critic in *Ratatouille* (2007) is known for his scathing write-ups of the restaurants he visits; however, in his mind, he merely believes that food should be a serious business, railing against Chef Gusteau's belief that anyone can cook. With *Inside Out 2*, just as Joy is always asking herself, as a willing chosen one should, 'How can I fix this?' so, too, is Anxiety. It is just that they have different ideas of what 'fixed' looks like for Riley. Anxiety almost goes on the same journey that Joy did in the first film, but this time as the antagonistic force.

As it was in the first film, the other original emotions (Anger, Sadness, Fear and Disgust) represent what Joy lacks as a chosen one and the blind spots to her skills. Although she has already gone through something of a transformation in the first film, she still presents an ego to the world that is further broken down with her journey through the dark forest to accept that although she has healed herself somewhat, there is still a long way for her to go before she can reach her full potential. Although the world of *Inside Out 2* appears to be incredibly complicated, and the mechanics of the plot are intricate, the piece remains at its core remarkably simple in that the emotions led by Joy must bring something back to their once upon a time to save the day. It is the complexity of their characters that actually makes for the real drama of the piece.

Finally, the clever dramatic construction of the hockey camp within the narrative becomes the ticking time bomb for our characters within Riley's mind. The camp creates an urgency to the dark forest that not only makes it harder to process the central conflict but also gives stakes to the situation as our characters and the audience need to see a resolution in a truncated timeline – something that gives urgency and dynamism to the narrative. Always be thinking in the narratives that you write: *Why does this problem have to be solved now? What would it mean if the dramatic situation isn't resolved before the conclusion of the narrative?*

Act 1: 'I'm a good person'

Our chosen one, Joy, 'operates' Riley from the console up in Headquarters as she plays a game of ice hockey, becoming something of a sports announcer for the action as it unfolds. This sequence is really important as it catches the audience up on the mechanics of the world of the film: emotions exist inside us and are able to dictate our actions by taking over the console at the centre of the Headquarters. It is a testament to the storytelling skills of the writers that they are able to explain such a complicated and intricate diegesis relatively easily in this brief sequence in an active and engaging way. Each of our supporting characters – Anger, Disgust, Fear and Sadness – are introduced as is their special skill when operating the console. It is clear that Joy is in charge up there and evidently always has the question 'How can I fix this?' at the front of her mind no matter the situation. From the first to the last minute of this film, Joy is a willing chosen one.

We then have Joy catch us up with what has happened since the last *Inside Out*. It is clear that the emotions have been keeping everything in tip-top shape. The personality islands that were so key to the last narrative are fully functional, and it is evident that Riley is growing up to be a well-adjusted, happy and thriving young person, as we would hope for our own children (and ourselves). We are introduced to the new 'beliefs' mechanic that informs everything to do with Riley's personality and helps construct her all-important 'sense of self', which is at the back of Headquarters. Beliefs are built from the memories that the emotions place within the Belief System, which is a small pool that exists just below Headquarters. Currently Riley's sense of self announces that Riley is a 'good person' if it is touched in a positive affirmation. However, on the horizon looms the fact that she is now moving into a new phase of her life: her teenage years.

Out in the real world, Riley's team win the big game that Joy has been narrating, and she is able to celebrate with her friends. This creates a new happy core memory. The high school hockey coach, Coach Roberts, then invites Riley and her best friends, Grace and Bree, to the hockey camp that she runs, something that both Riley and the emotions are very excited about. Riley and her friends agree.

Back in her bedroom with her parents, Riley has a sudden memory of the penalty that she incurred during the game and worries that maybe something similar will happen at the camp. Joy 'helpfully' stops the memory playing and instead launches it to the back of Riley's mind using a contraption that she has made herself so that she doesn't have to think about it anymore. This is Joy's constant answer to the question, 'How can I fix this?' Her ideology chimes completely with her name. She still wants more than anything to ensure that Riley is as blissfully happy as possible at all times, and that nothing should get in the way of her feeling this. She deliberately gets rid of all the memories that are unpleasant for Riley and ships all the others to her long-term memory. It wins her the accolades and respect of those around her who let her know that she is taking really good care of Riley.

Joy then takes Sadness to the Belief System so they can drop off one of the key memories they created from today about winning the game. As they do, they touch some of the threads, which rise up into the sky and inform Riley's sense of self. They are all further positive affirmations. This is a once upon a time that anyone would be happy to live in, all overseen and protected by Joy.

This huge amount of exposition is incredibly well handled by the writers. It catches us up in an active way with our characters, investigating the arena that they are in. Act 1 delivers all of the core information to a new audience without it feeling alienating to those who have an understanding of the broader mythology/lore of the franchise.

The invitation: Puberty inbound

The emotions wake up in the middle of the night to find that there is a new button on the console for 'Puberty'. As it begins ringing out, Joy launches it to the Back of the Mind in the hope that is the end of the matter. However, a group of workers arrive and begin to start tearing the place apart to start expanding Headquarters for 'the others'.

As Riley wakes up in the real world, Anger places a finger on the console causing Riley to shout at her mother. All of the other emotions do the same, resulting in the emergence of an extreme version of Riley. Anger blames the worker and what they have done to the console. It is clear that puberty is affecting Riley.

Ever the optimist, Joy attempts to fashion a contraption that keeps the emotions as far away from the console as possible but still allows them to operate it. Although this event is a clear interruption of identity for all those present, the once upon a time is not totally broken yet. Joy might be able to keep a handle on it using all of the skills that she has been using to cultivate Riley's current once upon a time. However, it is clear that we have entered into a new physical space and are at the fringes of the dark forest.

This sets in motion the various elements of the heart of the screenplay, which are:

- The path: To return Riley's sense of self after it has been shaken by the appearance of new emotions.
- Off the path: To understand that Joy doesn't have all the answers.
- The wolf: Anxiety, the new dominant emotion brought on by puberty.
- The suit of armour: Joy's unending enthusiasm and ability to go with the flow.
- The key/match: Riley's old sense of self.
- The gate: the console at Headquarters.

Act 2: 'I am such a huge fan of yours'

Riley then heads to hockey camp with her best friends. At Headquarters, Joy makes a rule that the emotions are only to touch the console if they absolutely need to. It is clear that Riley is really excited about the camp and is keen to impress the coach. We are also introduced to Valentina, or Val, who is the star on the current high school team that Riley hopes to be a part of and someone who Riley evidently aspires to be like.

At this point, Riley's friends let slip that this might be the last time they play on the same team together because they have been assigned to a different high school. It's evident that this has thrown Riley's world into disarray. However, the emotions hold strong and do not to touch the console until Riley has been dropped off. Sadness reaches out for the controls of the console for a moment before Joy pulls everything together suggesting that they will have plenty of time to think about this later.

Riley then runs right into Valentina and falls down, replicating a meet-cute of sorts that have occurred in countless films before. Val mistakenly says that Riley is from Michigan, something that Riley doesn't correct her about.

In Headquarters, the console turns orange, something it has never done before. We are then introduced to Anxiety. The world is now physically changing in a variety of ways both internally and externally. Anxiety races over and shakes Joy's hand, exclaiming that they are 'such a big fan'. They then introduce the other emotions that have come to join the original emotions in Riley's head. These are Envy, Embarrassment and Ennui, who each affect Riley in different ways.

Showing growth from the previous film, Joy accepts that these new emotions are obviously key to Riley's development and in a call-back to the adventure that she went on last time, gives Sadness a hug to remind us of the special friendship that the two have cultivated. Now, at the decisive moment where Riley could choose between her friends and her new life with Valentina, Anxiety takes the controls and points her in the direction of Valentina.

Joy and Anxiety argue about what this hockey camp should be about either as the last bonding moments with Riley's old friends or forging ahead with the supposed future that Riley has at her new high school. This directly sets up the conflict between Anxiety and Joy, showcasing their distinctive ideological outlooks and their respective answers to the central thematic and dramatic question at the heart of this story.

Anxiety showcases a variety of 'futures' that she predicts for Riley to justify why she has to take control of the console in order to save Riley from the potential humiliation of her first day of high school alone. Riley is then introduced to the other Firehawks at the camp who make up the high school hockey team that she would hope to join next year. When asked if Riley wants to sit with them, Joy makes her respond that she was going to save some seats for her friends. Anxiety worries that this decision will haunt them for the rest of their lives. This further compounds the conflict between how the pair of them respond to the central question. As their phones are being confiscated by the coach, Riley and her two older friends laugh behind her back as Joy has control of the console. This gets the whole team punished – something that causes everyone to lash out at them in the locker room. Back in Headquarters, it is clear that Joy is losing control of the situation and is going to have to work harder to fix this.

Out in the real world, Riley hears some of the girls talking about her while she is taking a drink break. The emotions turn to Joy for leadership, but instead Anxiety jumps in. She seeds the idea to Riley that if she is able to get Val on her side then everything will be fine. Driving the console, Anxiety has Riley talk to Val, who eventually takes her under her wing and says that the pair of them should be on the same team later on. Anxiety is then applauded by the other emotions for getting them out of this situation. Joy is losing yet more control of Headquarters to this new emotion. It also reinforces the idea that Anxiety is a planner in complete contrast to Joy, who is seemingly more freestyle in her approach.

Riley is then offered a distinctive choice between the team she should be on, either choosing to be with Grace and Bree or with Val and the Firehawks. Anxiety forces her to choose the latter over her old friends. To do this, she pulls Riley's sense of self off the pedestal it is on and, after a momentary tussle, fires it all the way to the Back of the Mind. Anxiety now has complete control over Riley as she tries to place the new anxious core memory into the Belief System to begin building a new sense of self for Riley that she believes will better serve her in this situation. When Joy, Anger, Fear, Sadness and Disgust try and stop them, Anxiety has Embarrassment bundle the old emotions into a jar and lower them out of Headquarters.

Anxiety then promises to change everything about Riley. She then starts the process of planting new anxious core memories into the Belief System that will build a new sense of self, starting with the one that echoes out: 'If I'm a Firehawk, I won't be alone.'

Act 3 (Part 1): Suppressed emotions

In the back of the police van, the original emotions are taken to the memory vault where they will be locked in. While they are there, they meet some of the secrets that Riley has locked away. They convince Riley's Deep Dark Secret to smash the jar that they are in and then call up Pouchy, who is a character from an animated children's show that Riley still secretly likes that resembles a yellow bumbag. In the bag, there is some TNT which Anger snatches and uses to blow a hole in the vault. The emotions then escape and, after a series of fortuitous circumstances, trap the guards in a cell of their own so they can make a clean getaway.

As they leave the Memory Bank, Anger wants to charge back to Headquarters, but Joy says that they have to go and find Riley's sense of self that currently is at the Back of the Mind. This, she hopes, will be the Match that will allow her to burn down the dark forest that Anxiety is currently in the process of cultivating. She convinces the other emotions to follow her despite their protests that she doesn't have a plan, and that Anxiety would ensure that there was a plan.

Joy then outlines her optimistic, if slightly naive, idea to rescue Riley and defeat Anxiety. This doesn't last long before it hits a road bump as the first corner they turn is actually a dead end, and it becomes increasingly clear that the old knowledge that Joy and Sadness have of this area of Riley's brain isn't useful anymore. However, they are then spurred on as it becomes evident that Riley has been woken up early by Anxiety to skate laps, and we are shown Riley's sense of self sinking lower into the pile of other memories that Joy has made her forget. The stakes are being raised. Anxiety pushes Riley hard on the ice, having her punish herself when she misses a shot. The other new emotions watch on, allowing them to take full control of the console. Val then appears and reinforces this rather negative behaviour to the emotions as a new core memory is created.

Back with the original emotions, Joy has managed to find the Stream of Consciousness, which she hopes they will be able to ride straight to the Back of the Mind. However, Sadness lets her know that someone has to be at the console to recall them up there. It becomes clear that Sadness is the only one who is able to do this because the other emotions aren't willing to, and Sadness is the only one who has read the manuals that explain would how to operate it. Sadness is strong-armed by Joy into the tube with a walkie-talkie in hand. This creates a nice little subplot and allows for Sadness to be active elsewhere in the narrative to create drama and tension.

At Headquarters, Anxiety takes yet more core memories down to the Belief System that further grows Riley's new sense of self, which is now spiky and orange rather than the pleasant blue it was before. There is now a real ticking clock. Her old sense of self slips further away in the pile of forgotten memories.

Riley is then introduced to the 'red notebook' that sits on the coach's desk. In it there are all of the thoughts that she has about the players in the camp. Envy and Anxiety wonder what might be written in there about Riley. Riley then heads to a party with the Firehawks where Riley is asked about her favourite band – an important rite of passage for any teenager. It's important that she gets this right. While trying to recall everything that Riley knows about music from the Back of the Mind, the new emotions also bring Sadness back into Headquarters where she is able to begin her part of the plan. Ennui manages to save the day with a sarcastic quip that breaks the Stream of Consciousness and stops Joy's most direct route to the Back of the Mind. Joy tries to enthuse the rest of the emotions to take the long way around, which they reluctantly agree to.

Midpoint: 'The Riley we know is gone'

Out in the real world, Riley learns about the impending scrimmage at the end of hockey camp which in previous years led to Val being picked for the team because she scored two goals. This sends Anxiety into overdrive, and she tries to accelerate her plan.

Unable to get to the next stage of her plan, Joy tries to get a better view of where they need to go. The other emotions appear to think that it is pointless to continue. As Disgust says, 'The Riley we know is gone.' Anger then calls Joy 'delusional'. This prompts a monologue where Joy is able to break down and admit that she doesn't have the answers and that maybe Anxiety is right that Riley doesn't need them anymore – something that makes her emotional.

It is now up to the other emotions to get her back on her feet and continue with the mission by getting her to see that her strengths are also her flaws. They have been momentarily forced off the path and now need to rally and get themselves back onto it. Anger grabs a vacuum that sends them to the top of the shelves so that they can more easily see the Back of the Mind, and they continue on the path.

Act 3 (Part 2): A new sense of self

Anxiety now doubles down on her plan to get Riley on the team. Meanwhile, Embarrassment uncovers Sadness's hiding spot but keeps her secret actually hiding her further behind the wall of folders she is building.

Anxiety takes over the workers in Imaginationland and uses them to create visions of what might go wrong for Riley tomorrow. Joy tries to combat this with the other emotions by sending positive projections into the mix. Anxiety recognizes that this is happening and calls her out. Joy rallies the other workers in Imaginationland to fill Riley's head with positive ideas and eventually to stop them all together so that Riley can sleep. This is the first time since their separation that the pair are now in direct conflict, and their two differing ideologies are on display in fighting through the central question. The Mind Police arrive, and the emotions escape.

Anxiety takes control of the console and makes Riley head to the coach's office to see what is written about her in the notebook. Sadness talks to Joy on the walkie-talkies and is given the responsibility of stopping this. She bravely finds Ennui's remote control and operates the console, preventing Riley from reading the book … for the moment. Her plan is discovered, and Aniexty takes the console back to have Riley see that the coach has written that Riley isn't ready yet. This makes Anxiety resolute that they have one day left to change coach's mind. This causes a brainstorm that not only means that Joy believes that the emotions must stop the bad ideas reaching Riley but also impedes their progress towards Headquarters as the ideas rain down on them.

Anxiety calls up a big idea as he believes that none of the other ideas are good enough. Still determined to make sure that as many of them don't reach Headquarters as possible, Joy tries to prevent it from getting there. However, Fear says that it is also their only way to get themselves out of the situation they are in by clinging on to the idea and riding it out of the brainstorm. Joy is now offered an impossible choice, and she relinquishes control and travels with the idea out of the storm. As the emotions land safely, they set back off up to the Back of the Mind.

Act 4: 'I'm not good enough'

Riley dyes her hair with the distinctive red flash of a Firehawk. Anxiety decides that Riley will need to score three goals to be on the team and travels back down to the Belief System to finally complete Riley's new sense of self filled with the orange of anxiety.

Joy and the old emotions arrive at the mountain of memories that Joy has sent to the Back of the Mind. It is more than she has previously remembered sending there (a hint to the realization that she is about to make), and she and the emotions climb to reach Riley's old sense of self at the top. As she grabs it, the affirmation, 'I'm a good person' completely fades as the new one in Headquarters completes itself, and the phrase 'I'm not good enough' rings out, surprising everyone present, including Anxiety. This is a very literal change in psychological outlook for Riley and the other characters present, who now must react to this brave new world they are experiencing both for Riley and themselves.

Embarrassment frees Sadness so that she is able to bring Joy and the other emotions into Headquarters from the Back of the Mind. She operates the console, but it's too late: Anxiety destroys the tube that would bring them back, and they are now trapped at the Back of the Mind.

Lost and unable to return, the emotions turn to Joy, asking what their next move will be. Joy has no idea currently and turns away from them. Joy falls to her knees and inspects the memories that she has sent to the Back of the Mind. She cries, pleading that there must be something that she is missing. She cradles Riley's old sense of self and is finally able to admit that she doesn't know what to do and that she has no plan to stop Anxiety, and that feeling less joy is a sad but inevitable part of growing up. However, she is steely in her resolve and knows that they must find a plan for the sake of Riley.

The scrimmage at camp starts, and Riley is now entirely driven by the mantra that she isn't good enough – a direct contrast to the balance of emotions who assisted her in playing and enjoying hockey at the beginning of the piece. Although this appears to work at first, with Riley scoring a goal, there is evidently something brewing at Headquarters that will mean this will not last.

Atop the mountain of discarded memories, Anger encourages the emotions to call for Pouchy from earlier. As he starts his riddle for what might help them, Anger jams his hand into his mouth and grabs the dynamite to use in their plan. Anxiety encourages Riley to take the puck from her own teammates out in the real world in the pursuit of her own desires to be the best.

Joy then convinces the emotions to blow up the mountain and ride all of the bad memories back to Headquarters. Disgust worries that the bad memories might form bad beliefs, but Joy is determined to try and make this work. She has to relinquish control and allow this to happen so that Riley can achieve what she wants. They push the plunger. The dynamite explodes, and the first part of the plan is working. Out on the ice, Anxiety pushes Riley too hard, and she ends up hurting Grace. Riley is sent to the penalty box as she feared that she would in the beginning of the narrative. Riley begins to have a panic attack as Anxiety overwhelms the console.

Joy arrives in the Belief System with all the memories that begin to sink into the water there. It's clear that Riley is now having an anxiety attack. Anxiety forms a cloud around the console, blocking it from everyone else. Joy approaches and is able to break through …

The last throw of the dice: 'Anxiety, stop!'

Joy enters into the fray to find that Anxiety is standing, paralysed, at the controls of the console. Joy tells Anxiety, 'You don't get to decide who Riley is.' However, she realizes that Anxiety is only experiencing what Joy did in the first film. She heaves her off the console and is finally able to replace Riley's sense of self with the one that she has been carrying this whole time.

Anxiety finally realizes her mistake: that none of them are able to choose who Riley is. Joy understands her own conflicted nature better as we flash back to her sending all the bad memories to the Back of the Mind. She must learn from these mistakes just as Anxiety does.

All of the memories in the Belief System form together and come up to Headquarters. Joy rips the sense of self from the pedestal that she has carried from the Back of the Mind, and a new sense of self forms for Riley which is complicated and messy with all of the emotions represented in their various colours. Riley is not one thing: she is multiple things. Joy hugs this version of Riley, and all the other emotions pile in after her to embrace her sense of self. This calms her in the real world and stops her panic attack.

Riley reaches out and touches the bench and is reminded why she loves hockey. Her friends approach her, realizing that she is in distress, and ask if she is okay. She confesses that she been worried since they told her that they were going to another school and apologizes for her poor behaviour. They do as well, and the friends embrace.

Act 5: 'Riley wants you, Joy'

Riley basks in the glow of the sun, and, in Headquarters, the console is calling for Joy. This is the reward for her finally being able to fix things and a spiritual affirmation that what she has done is right. Riley smiles and enjoys playing hockey as Joy works the controls. The other emotions watch on.

We arrive at the high school where Riley is waiting to see if she has been chosen on the team. Anxiety worries about the repercussions of Riley not being picked. However, Joy is able to calm her down. Riley's phone buzzes, and her old friends send a good-luck message. Everything is back to how it should be in this new version of Riley's once upon a time. The emotions share how much they love Riley, even given some of her less perfect traits. Riley stands at her locker looking into the mirror. She gets a message, pulls up her phone, looks in the mirror, and we … cut to black.

It is an ambiguous ending that still offers catharsis: the lingering image of a world where a dark forest has been burnt and from whose ashes a new one can be created.

8

Unknowing case study The Fall Guy (2024)

Logline: A down-and-out Hollywood stuntman is tasked with finding the star of his ex-girlfriend's blockbuster movie while trying to win back the girl of his dreams
Release date: 3 May 2024
Screenplay: Glen A. Larson and Drew Pearce

Following the phenomenal success of *Barbie*, someone in Hollywood must have thought they had a potentially massive hit on their hands by conjuring up a Ryan Gosling/Emily Blunt romantic comedy based on an established 1980s TV show. However, people in Hollywood sometimes make strange decisions, and, somehow or other, nobody steps in to correct that strange decision until millions upon millions of dollars have been spent and the studio is left with a film of questionable qualities on their hands.

A romantic comedy set in the testosterone-fuelled world of stunt men where quotes from *The Fast and the Furious* vie with touching scenes of Ryan Gosling crying in a car while listening to Taylor Swift make for odd bedfellows and an even more confused view of who the core audience for this film might be. The film made a profit, largely on the back of its starry cast, and it does contain some memorable comic moments and some eye-popping action scenes, but, more importantly for this book, as a tent-pole Hollywood blockbuster release, it closely tracks the unknowing story pathway and, as such, is a useful case study in mainstream film-making for a wide audience that effectively follows the rules of one of our key paradigms. We would also argue that sometimes you can learn a lot more from a film that doesn't do everything right than from films that do.

Prologue: Too much face

We are introduced to stuntman Colt Seavers and his girlfriend, camera operator Jody Moreno, on the set of a big action movie where Colt is working as a stunt double for big movie star Tom Ryder. The film's producer, Gail Meyer, urges Colt to repeat a dangerous stunt as there was 'too much face' in the shot. Colt must perform the stunt backwards to avoid being identified as Ryder's double. Following some interplay between Colt and Jody, where it is clear that they are a close and happy couple, Colt performs the stunt, and all cuts to black as screams echo across the lot. The stunt has gone desperately wrong.

Act 1: 'You need to be smashing burning Kawasakis'

Eighteen months later, and we rejoin Colt. A voice-over fills us in on the information that Colt has disappeared from the lives of all of his co-workers, friends and, crucially, Jody. He is now working as a valet at a Mexican restaurant, where he receives a phone call from Gail, who asks him to take on the role of stuntman on the latest Tom Ryder vehicle, *Metalstorm*.

Colt refuses outright, but then Gail tells him that the film's director is Jody, working on her first movie, and she's asked specifically for Colt to be taken on. Still holding a candle for Jody, Colt accepts the offer. However, arriving on set in Sydney and meeting up with old friend, stunt coordinator Dan Tucker, it is very quickly apparent that not only has Jody not asked for Colt specifically, but she doesn't even know he is on set. It is also revealed that she is having problems with the third act of the film.

As we have seen, the unknowing story path is often made up of not just one bargain or unfair deal but potentially many. This first deal that Colt accepts is not the deal that will carry the drama of the film forward but is a stepping stone towards the invitation. By using the notion of the unfair bargain throughout the unknowing narrative, the writer can create a world in which the chosen one is used and exploited, not just by the wolf in the story but by any number of characters they meet along the way. The unknowing chosen one must learn to recognize that they are prone to exploitation through the course of the story, but this realization will often only occur at the very end of the narrative, at the moment where they decide to finally be honest with themselves and discover the key that will unlock the second gate.

When Colt finally meets up with Jody face to face, the meeting is not what he expected it to be. She has been deeply hurt by the fact that Colt ghosted her following his accident, and, in fact, the plot of *Metalstorm* is an attempt for Jody to overcome the hurt of the break-up. Jody makes it very clear that she does not want Colt on the set; however, there are no other stuntmen available and so another uneasy deal is made in which Colt must do what his director tells him to … and Jody clearly wants to hurt him, forcing him to perform the same dangerous, painful stunt over and over as she tells him the story of the central characters of her film, Aliena and Space Cowboy, which closely mirrors the break-up between Colt and Jody following his accident. A very public conversation takes place in front of cast and crew, ostensibly regarding *Metalstorm* but actually about what happened between Colt and Jody at the end of which Colt apologizes for his disappearance.

The invitation: Find Tom Ryder

Colt then confronts producer Gail about her lie. Gail admits to the 'real' reason behind her wanting Colt to join the shoot: Tom Ryder has fallen in with some shady people and has gone missing. Gail wants Colt to find him; otherwise, the shoot will collapse, and *Metalstorm* will be Jody's first and last film. This is an archetypal unknowing invitation in that it appears to be a fairly simple task well within the capabilities of the chosen one. The deal carries with it a 'What if?' in that if Colt refuses the invitation, worse things will happen. He does not particularly want to sign up to the deal, but, at this point in the story, the stakes do not seem to be particularly high for him. The invitation, crucially, is easy for him to accept. However, fully in keeping with all unknowing chosen ones, he doesn't fully understand what he is signing up to, but the question that all unknowing chosen ones must ask themselves is now hanging over the piece: 'How do I get out of this?' Colt is only completing the deal with Gail so that he can support Jody in her directorial debut. He has no emotional investment in the task ahead and just wants it to be over.

It is interesting to note that we are now thirty minutes into a two-hour film, and the invitation has only just been delivered. In unknowing narratives, we often find that there is an extended prologue sequence prior to the first act and the delivery of the invitation. We are thirty-seven pages into the screenplay of *Jojo Rabbit* before Jojo makes his deal with Elsa. We are twenty pages into the screenplay of *Shrek* (2001) before Lord Farquaad makes his deal with Shrek. We are over twenty pages into the script of *Pretty Woman* before Edward asks Vivian to stay with him for the week.

The extended prologue makes sense in the context of the unknowing narrative. We must not only establish a clear once upon a time for the chosen one, but we must also establish a dramatic trajectory for them. When we first meet them, they must be set upon a path of action that will be subverted by the delivery of the invitation. The deal they are offered will, initially at least, be a diversion from their main focus, but will unexpectedly take them over when they realize that they have been duped into accepting the invitation because they have not been in possession of all of the facts. The invitation on the unknowing story arc is either delivered by the disruptor, the character who will change the direction of the chosen one's story path, or by the wolf, the character who will be tricking the chosen one into accepting the deal. The wolf, however, does not normally make themselves known until the second half of the film, as we will see …

Colt's trajectory in *The Fall Guy* is very clearly focused on the reignition of his relationship with Jody. That is what he is seeking when Gail steps in and diverts him. Her diversion is related to his main aim in that by finding Ryder he will also be helping Jody complete her film, but it will also disrupt his efforts to woo her directly. As an example of an unknowing invitation, this is effective and credible. The chosen one is torn between two story paths and decides to, briefly, accept a challenge that is supposed to act as a temporary diversion but will turn out to be much more. When building this diversion, you must fully consider the consequences of this course of action for your chosen one because they will only escape the dark forest by fully embracing this deal and recognizing that, far from being a diversion, it is the challenge that will help them to grow and change as a character and achieve the aim that has eluded them on the main story path. Crucially, the answer to the question 'How do I get out of this?' will change as the chosen one's eyes are opened to the true nature of the dark forest.

Here, the mechanics of the film to come are laid bare, and the potential shortcomings in the narrative are signposted:

- The path: Colt must regain Jody's trust if they are ever to become a couple again/Jody must find Tom Ryder. Both of these paths are, initially at least, almost entirely separate.
- off the path: Colt must understand that the only way to get Jody back is through honesty and openness.
- The wolf: ... will be revealed in the second half of the film.
- The suit of armour: Colt's stuntman abilities, which will be enough to solve the Tom Ryder story but not enough to win the girl.
- The key: Colt's final expressions of truth and honesty towards Jody.
- The gate: Jody's acceptance of Colt's love for her.

Act 2: 'Save Jody's movie, and maybe you'll get the love of your life back'

The Fall Guy is not a subtle film. Dialogue signposts the direction of the story throughout, and, while this can feel a little clunky and formulaic in the context of the story, for the script analyst, attempting to identify the framework of the narrative in order to lay bare the mechanics of the story, this can be incredibly useful. Drew Pearce, by the way, is a talented writer with some laudable credits to his name, including *Iron Man 3* (2013) and *Mission Impossible: Rogue Nation*

(2015), but the process of script development in Hollywood does not always gel effectively with the creation of great art.

There are bright, imaginative, sparky moments throughout the film, displaying Pearce's skills as a writer and the actors' abilities to bring their characters to life, but at times the film itself seems to be struggling to understand exactly what it is. Even the notion of the unresolved third act feels real, as if the film-makers themselves have not figured out the third act as they labour their way through the plot.

Having said that, Colt accepts the deal, and the path before him is absolutely clear, as it should be in the unknowing narrative. He wears his suit of armour for all to see. He is a stuntman capable of amazing feats of physical endurance and skill, and the task before him – to find Ryder and return him to the set of *Metalstorm* – should be simple.

Colt accesses Ryder's apartment and is immediately attacked by his girlfriend, Iggy Starr, wielding a sword. The engagement is light and fun because Colt is a stuntman and can deal with this kind of thing. Following a fight sequence, Iggy tells Colt that Ryder 'is really drugged up and paranoid' and gives him a lead: his drug dealer Doone. As an aside, introducing peripheral characters who only exist to deliver information to further the plot is never a display of writing prowess ... but we digress ...

Colt heads straight to a club to seek out Doone. The path is short, and the gate is in sight. Why waste time? However, this is an unfair deal, and the path is about to get more difficult to negotiate. Doone drugs Colt, and a fight/chase sequence ensues ending in Doone admitting that he was paid to drug Colt by the guy that runs Ryder's security, Dressler. Doone regularly delivers drugs to Dressler at the Pendleton Hotel, which is where Colt heads next, still firmly on the path, still stoically wearing his suit of armour, still not engaging with the real narrative of *The Fall Guy*: his relationship with Jody.

In order to keep this side of the story going, Colt bumps into Jody at the hotel, and they have an awkward conversation, but the relationship between them is continuing to thaw as they joke together. Once again, Jody asks Colt why he disappeared for a year, and, once again, Colt apologizes. Also, once again, the unresolved third act of *Metalstorm* is raised before Colt finds himself heading back on the path in his search for Ryder as he is directed to the room in the hotel which Ryder's security guy uses for his drug deliveries.

The somewhat awkward marrying of romantic comedy and action picture is laid bare in these scenes as the narrative is pulled in two different directions simultaneously and the action picture wins out. Jody and Colt really don't have very much to talk about at this stage in the screenplay. Their only topic of conversation is an attempt to understand and potentially patch up their problems in the past, and, as Jody has no knowledge of Ryder's disappearance, she currently has no investment in the unfolding dramatic narrative and so her appearances in the narrative tend to slow the forward motion of the drama rather than add to it. Jody has no investment in the plot right now.

The plot of *The Fall Guy* could not be accused of being complex, but it does fail the simplicity test in that it is being dragged in two directions and there is no central dramatic focus to the piece. Do we care more about the relationship or the conspiracy? The danger is that we care about neither if the focus is not clear.

With the aid of a contact at the hotel, Colt makes his way to the room mentioned by Doone. His search of the room is interrupted by a call from Jody regarding the unresolved third act of *Metalstorm*. The conversation once again mirrors the difficulties of their own relationship based on Colt's disappearance, and the conversation, as before, slows down the forward motion of the narrative. There are imaginative and characterful elements to this sequence as the use of split screen enhances the conversation, but their shared dilemma does not move forward, and the sequence acts to interrupt the ongoing conspiracy plot, ending with no resolution just before Colt discovers a dead body in the hotel-room bath.

Act 3 (Part 1): 'I don't need anything. I just need you … to finish this movie'

Colt calls Gail about the dead body, and Gail urges him not to call the police or the shoot will be shut down. The dark forest has just got darker, but the path is still clearly in front of Colt. Despite Gail's protestations, he calls the police in, but the body has mysteriously disappeared. Ryder is still missing, the film is still in jeopardy, and Colt still has a job to do.

Back on set, Jody has had an epiphany following the split-screen phone conversation the previous night. She is planning to have Colt film all of Ryder's scenes and replace his face with Ryder's. Colt is suddenly essential to the movie. Plus, Jody is planning a 250-foot jump in a truck, which will provide the action she has been missing in the third act. It's not entirely clear how this dangerous stunt will resolve the relationship between Aliena and Space Cowboy nor how it has anything to do with the previous night's phone conversation, but Jody says it will help the film so let's just go with it. Crucially, the relationship between Jody and Colt has warmed up considerably, and, after a successful action-shooting sequence, Jody invites Colt to a karaoke bar with other members of the cast and crew.

Unexpectedly, Gail moves in on Colt following Jody's departure and tells him that she made a mistake in employing him on the film and has bought him a plane ticket out of there. Colt decides to ignore Gail's ticket and to track down Ryder's personal assistant, Alma Milan instead. He also has that karaoke invitation to consider. At this point, Colt's 'How do I get out of here?' question is getting slightly fuzzy. He has been offered a way out but turns it down. There is still his relationship with Jody to consider here so, once again, let's accept the decision and move on, while recognizing that the film's diversions from the rules and tools we suggest in this book are not necessarily strengthening the storytelling.

As a moment in the film where the action storyline and the romantic plot align, this is one of the more successful. Colt wants to meet up with Jody in the karaoke bar, and that is his main focus attention, but the action narrative is impeding that desire. For the first time, the balance between the storylines seems to be working correctly. Colt's relationship with Jody is more emotionally important to him and to the audience than the search for Ryder.

Colt heads back to Ryder's apartment and meets up with Alma, who reveals that she has Ryder's phone which both he and Gail have been searching for. They also meet up with Jean Claude, a stunt dog that Colt has previously worked with on films. Jean Claude will prove very useful in a series of upcoming action set pieces. Shortly after Alma hands over the locked phone, they are attacked by Dressler and the security team. Another long action sequence ensues intercut with Jody at the karaoke bar, and expecting Colt to join her there. As the action ramps up, Jody learns from Gail that Colt has taken a plane back the USA, and she sings a sad Phil Collins number. Meanwhile, Colt travels across the city battling bad guys in a garbage truck.

Midpoint: The path has disappeared …

Eventually, Colt gets away with the phone and heads to the bar, but Jodi has already left. There he meets up with his old friend, stunt coordinator Dan and shares the fact that he has Ryder's phone, which they need to open if they're going to discover where he is. Together they decide to head back to Ryder's apartment to find a clue to the phone's passcode, which they discover and open the phone. There they find a video that shows a drunken Ryder inadvertently killing his last stunt double, Henry: the body from the bath in the Pendleton Hotel.

At this point, they also find out that the body at the Pendleton has now been discovered … along with CCTV footage showing Colt entering the hotel room. Colt's face has been deep-faked onto the real murderer's body, and he is being framed for the murder of Henry. Colt and Dan have the video proof that he is innocent.

As a midpoint, these events are effective in revealing new information to Colt and incriminating him in a murder he didn't commit. Beyond these useful complicating elements, however, if we consider the path and the gate, then we have reached a classic moment in an unknowing narrative: just as the chosen one approaches the gate so that they can exit the story, it becomes clear that the deal was unfair and there is a much larger, much more dangerous dark forest beyond the first gate which they must traverse off the path. The original deal, that Colt find Ryder and persuade him to return to the film, has now been usurped by a more urgent requirement for Colt: to clear himself of a murder accusation. The path has disappeared, the gate has evaporated, and Colt's suit of armour is suddenly of little use to him. His only option is to head off the path if he is going to undo this deal and return to his once upon a time with Jody.

It is interesting to note that there are no 'midpoint moments' with regards to the Colt/Jody plotline. All of the attention is, once again, on Ryder, and the romantic story is tangential. When you have two storylines pulling against each other, the danger is that one of them becomes a distraction and an irritant rather than each acting as dramatic props holding one another up. Jody pulls Colt away from the action storyline; the action storyline pulls Colt away from Jody. There is no synergy between the two, and the action storyline wins out.

Act 3 (Part 2): High noon at the edge of the universe

Once again, Dressler and the bad guys move in on Colt as he and Dan try to escape Ryder's apartment. The phone with the incriminating video is destroyed in the shoot-out, and Dan gets away while Colt is taken by the bad guys. He finds himself tied to a chair on a yacht confronted by none other than Ryder himself who demands Colt return the incriminating phone.

Here we finally discover the identity of the wolf in this film. Wolves in unknowing storylines often take a while to identify themselves, and this identification normally, if not always, comes after the first gate. As the chosen one realizes that the deal they have agreed to is unfair and the gate they thought would end their ordeal disappears, so the wolf is revealed … in the second half of the film. In this case, the wolf is Gail. While Ryder is definitely a bad guy and responsible for the death of Henry, it is Gail who is pulling the strings here, framing Colt for the murder and trying to cover up Ryder's misdemeanours.

When Jody discovers that Colt didn't get on the plane, all of the elements are in place for the relationship to fall back into place, but she doesn't realize that Colt is currently in mortal danger. Once again, the romantic story and the action story are aligning more closely and effectively in this moment. Back at the boat, with Colt tied to a chair and Ryder monologuing, it comes out that Colt's accident at the beginning of the film was no accident. Ryder scuppered the stunt to teach Colt a lesson. He'd got 'too big for his boots'. Now they are going to have to change the plan from framing Colt for the murder of Henry to a murder–suicide scenario in which they kill Colt. Following this stand-off between Colt and Ryder, Colt admits that the phone has been destroyed, and, consequently, Ryder orders his security men to kill Colt.

Another action sequence ensues intercut with Jody's realization that Colt has been accused of murder and her assertion that she believes in his innocence.

She is finally being pulled wholeheartedly into the central storyline of the film, and, consequently, the relationship between her and Colt is beginning to take centre stage in a film that, until this point, has been pulled towards the action sequences rather than the emotional heart of the narrative: the relationship between Colt and Jody.

Time for another high-octane, testosterone-fuelled action sequence ending in a speedboat chase during which Colt manages to phone Jody when he finally digs deep, admitting to her that, following his accident, which wasn't an accident, he disappeared because he realized he wasn't invincible and thought that Jody wouldn't be attracted to him anymore as a result. As heartfelt confessions go, it's not that deep, but Colt's only a stuntman so maybe his feelings run shallow. However, this confession does do what unknowing chosen ones must do in order to secure the key to open the second gate; it is the point at which Colt sheds his suit of armour and realizes that the stuntman in him is not going to land the girl. This is his own personal answer to the 'How do I get out of this?' question. Only honesty and the realization that he isn't invincible will do that. Not ideal, but serviceable and a handy way to carry us into the low point of the film at the end of the act as the sequence concludes with the apparent death of Colt in a massive explosion that segues into news reports of the suicide of the man responsible for Henry's death.

Act 4: 'All we have left is the alien truck coverage'

Of course, Colt isn't dead. His stuntman suit of armour is still good for something. He sneaks onto the set of *Metalstorm* and dons an alien costume so he can make his way into Jody's Winnebago to speak with her. After a brief fight, Jody tells Colt to run. She will cover for him. To hell with *Metalstorm*. Colt, however, has other plans. With him supposedly dead, he predicts that Ryder will return to finish the movie, and he really wants Jody to finish her movie.

At this point, Gail knocks on the Winnebago door, and Colt warns Jody that she is in on it. With Colt hiding in the bathroom, Gail commiserates with Jody about Colt's death and tells him that Ryder is returning to finish the film, as Colt predicted. However, they won't be able to do the 'impossible jump' without Colt. Ryder will, however, be able to deliver Jody's new 'bombastic monologue' for the final act.

The last throw of the dice: impossible jump

When Gail leaves, Jody and Colt decide that they can both finish the movie and clear his name: by miking Ryder up and getting him to confess while they do the 'impossible jump'. The plan isn't particularly clear if we are honest. Why they need to do the jump, and why this is intrinsically linked to Ryder's confession, is anybody's guess, but that's the way they've decided to send the audience home satisfied so, once again, let's go with it and head into the fifth and final act …

Act 5: Spicy margaritas and bad decisions

With buy-in from Dan and the crew, the plan is put into action. Colt gets into the car with Tom as they head towards the jump. As soon as Gail realizes this is a set-up, Dressler and the security guys attempt to stop them, but there are all kinds of explosions and what have you rigged to stop this from happening. During the race towards the jump, Colt manages to get Ryder to confess on mic that the brains behind the whole plan, such as it is, was Gail.

Colt and Ryder survive the spectacular jump, but Gail hasn't given up yet. She heads down to the sound truck and steals the hard drive with the confession on it. She then calls in a helicopter to take her to safety. Don't ask.

More spectacular stunts as the helicopter takes off and Colt manages to leap aboard, grappling with Ryder, Gail and the hard drive as the helicopter sways through the skies and the crew below, led by Dan drag a big airbag/crash mat around trying to place it beneath the helicopter so that Colt can jump to safety. Eventually this happens, and the hard drive is secured. We cut to a time in the future when *Metalstorm* has been released, with Jason Momoa in the lead, and it's been a huge hit. Colt and Jody are together, and we have a happy ending on our hands.

The ending of *The Fall Guy* represents a number of fun action sequences strung together in order to tie up the loose ends and bring the story home for the audience, but, in all honesty, it's not that emotionally satisfying. This is really because the writers have missed an important element of the unknowing chosen one's story arc, in that there will be a final moment of digging extra deep to really enable the growth, self-realization and understanding to allow the chosen one to embrace their future as a knowing chosen one who has undone the deal and created a new once upon a time. There is no such moment here. Colt's confession to Jody is delivered over the phone, and there are no real deep revelations or understandings to glean from that moment. The final act rests, once again, on pyrotechnics rather than emotional depth. Jody's character remains as shallow as it was at the beginning, and Colt has put his suit of armour back on again.

If we take a moment to consider our all-important formula for effective storytelling – *Simple story, complex characters* – *The Fall Guy* falls down on both counts. The story ricochets from event to event with no strong central dramatic/emotional core holding it together. The film-makers seem more intent on cooking up exciting action sequences than having those sequences further the emotional story in a satisfying way. Colt and Jody are not particularly complex characters. They have issues to resolve, but these issues are all centred on a single moment: the failed stunt. We learn nothing more about them as people. We have nothing to invest in or empathize with. They are not like us, they are like movie stars going through the motions.

The Fall Guy is full of interesting moments and grasps the unknowing narrative arc to a degree but never quite overcomes the pull between the two different storylines, action and romantic, which gel as one. The cartoonish villainy of the wolf does not allow the chosen one to really grasp the importance of honesty above action, and the film-makers' preference for action above romance creates, in Jody, a thin and ineffectual character who does little to participate in the story.

If you are developing an unknowing narrative then it is so valuable to watch an example of a story on this arc that doesn't quite pay off in order for you to recognize what you need to place into your screenplay to really make it sing, and you could do worse than watching *The Fall Guy*.

9

Unable-to-believe case study Barbie (2023)

Logline: When Barbie starts experiencing dark thoughts, she is sent to the real world to discover what it is like to live there and how she might be able to help fix it.

Release: 21 July 2023

Screenwriters: Greta Gerwig and Noah Baumbach

Based on the wildly popular IP from Mattel, *Barbie* has evidently been created by someone who has a solid understanding of how the brand wants to communicate their image within the film. How Barbie moves, thinks, acts and reacts is built with an awareness in mind of the experiences that many will have had playing with the toy when they were younger but also has a reflective irony to it that the target millennial audience enjoys. This is also true of other massive IP projects such as *The Lego Movie* (2014), which did something similar, and arguably has a similar narrative structure. A key lesson for those who are pitching on projects with broad appeal in the future is to understand the initial audience of these pieces and how they relate to the property that you are adapting.

The narrative to the piece does wander slightly from time to time, and it is testament to the writing partnership of Gerwig and Baumbach that they are able to orient us back onto the central path of the narrative quickly and effectively when they are required to. As with all Gerwig's work, the place women hold within society is explored throughout the narrative, as is the relationship between mothers and their daughters. The central dramatic relationships have an authenticity to them that allows for characters to explore the key themes and ideas of the piece in engaging and interesting ways. The overall plot is a simple one, but the conflicted natures the characters exhibit ensure that the solutions are not easy to achieve.

The functions of the mentor figure, which are so key to this paradigm, are shared widely amongst many characters within the narrative. This is a rather fitting idea for this piece as it chimes with the broader thematic ideas of how there are a multitude of different models of womanhood in the twenty-first century and each need to cherish and support one another. It is also, once again, smart writing from Gerwig and Baumbach that ensures that, at the key dramatic turning points, the primary mentor figure is kept close to the action.

Just as a note, with all of the characters in the piece basically sharing the same first name, it is often difficult to differentiate them. One of the first 'rules' of screenwriting is to make sure that each of your characters have names that start with different letters (partly because of Final Draft's predictive text function). This one evidently went out of the window very early in the writing process ... We hope that it is relatively clear who we are talking about during the chapter. We have tried to make it as easy to understand as possible.

Prologue: A cultural sensation

Barbie sets out its stall early in this section of the narrative with a *2001: A Space Odyssey* (1968) pastiche that alerts us to the cultural sensation that the character of Barbie is and how she broke the zeitgeist of toys for girls. This clearly sets the tone and broader thematic ideas that the piece is going to be developing on during its runtime. The pastiche element of this sequence is also a smart one as it elevates the piece away from being the solely classical cinematic work that it could have been. We are barely five minutes in, and our expectations have been challenged and subverted quickly and effectively.

Act 1: 'Do you guys ever think about dying?'

This subversion continues into the first act of the piece where Barbie's history is condensed, and potentially overly simplified, to ally her with the thematic underpinning of the piece. Her accomplishments are given a progressive spin, and she emerges as a champion for women's rights, female empowerment and inclusion. Because Barbie can be anything, this means that women can be anything.

We also have the rules of how Barbie Land and the real world interact with one another explained to us. This is, of course, a utopian and idealized version of how these mechanics work, and the narration over the top of this claiming that Barbie has ushered in a new age of equal rights very much has the twinge of the ironic over the top finishing up with: 'at least that's what the Barbies think …' We have a clear and concise once upon a time that is soon going to be shattered as our chosen one approaches the acceptance of her invitation.

The typical day for our chosen one unfolds in a world where nothing bad ever happens. She literally floats out of her house into her car and drives down the street without a care in the world. The setting around her does a large amount of storytelling with everything that distinctive shade of Barbie pink. She fits into it perfectly with her dress which is exactly the same colour. Her once upon a time is made for her, and she is made for it.

Among the frivolous things we see, Barbie has also achieved so much in her world with a variety of characters winning Nobel Prizes and even Lawyer Barbie seemingly passing a motion at the Barbie Supreme Court to overturn Citizens United and get big money out of Barbie politics. However, our Barbie seems to be on the fringes of most of the larger decisions and merely watches on as they unfold. She is, after all, stereotypical Barbie, and these ideas are not something that she should be getting involved with.

We are then introduced to (the first) Ken who seemingly exists at this moment only to be within Barbie's orbit. While at the beach, he is desperate to get Barbie's attention. After charging towards the plastic waves, he ends up being tossed into the air and hurting himself. His rival, Ken, squares up to him and threatens to 'beach him off'. After he has received treatment in the mobile hospital that the Barbies have set up for him, Ken boldly asks if he can come to Barbie's house tonight, crossing his fingers for good luck. She agrees.

The Barbies, Ken(s) and Alan then all have a big party in Barbie's cul-de-sac. Here it is again clear that the Kens are attempting to compete for Barbie's attention, setting up this conflict that will become a core part of the narrative as it unfolds. The world is momentarily interrupted when Barbie blurts out, 'Do you guys ever think about dying?' A literal record scratch accompanies this, and she quickly retracts it, pushing her initial thought down saying, 'I'm just dying to dance.' Everyone carries on as normal, but it is clear from Barbie's pained expression that there is something wrong with her … a conflicted nature that she is unable to fully express. After the party, Ken then tries to get a goodnight kiss, something that Barbie refuses. She then heads into her Dreamhouse for girls' night, leaving him dejected.

As Barbie wakes up the next morning, it is clear that she isn't feeling as perfect as normal with her even falling off the roof of her house. This sequence culminates in her feet falling flat to the floor. Something that all of the Barbies (and some Kens) find repugnant. All of them agree that Barbie is malfunctioning and needs to go and discuss things with Weird Barbie, our mentor figure. She is introduced as a character who a little girl in the real world played with too hard, and we are shown this in a montage. As a wizened character who has advanced knowledge of the real world and the mechanics of Barbie Land, she will have the answers.

The invitation: A choice of shoes

Weird Barbie then diagnoses Barbie's thoughts of death as something that has opened a portal between Barbie Land and the real world. She will have to go to the real world and find the girl who is playing with her and fix this. Weird Barbie believes that the girl who is playing with her is sad, and this emotion is being transferred onto Barbie.

Barbie then confesses that she has only ever wanted everything to stay exactly as it is. She also believes, wrongly, that the world is a perfect place for women, and she has had something to do with the creation of this utopia. She also doesn't understand how her little girl could be sad. Weird Barbie then sets out the stakes, suggesting that if Barbie cannot fix the issue at hand, then what is ugly will become uglier and what is weird will become weirder. Tellingly, Weird Barbie then directly tells Barbie that she believes in her … a direct sign of the paradigm we are dealing with here. There is more in her than merely being stereotypical Barbie.

Barbie is then offered a choice between two sets of shoes: her regular heels or a pair of Birkenstocks. Barbie of course refuses as all unable-to-believe chosen ones should. However, her mentor pushes the 'correct' choice on her and sends her off into the real world. Shoes are a central motif not only within the narrative of Barbie but also within one of the key models for the unable-to-believe narratives, Cinderella. Various elaborate modes of transport are laid before Barbie in order to transport her into the real world, and she is on her way. Weird Barbie will be Barbie's primary mentor as the one who understands the kind of adventure Barbie will be going on and the path that Barbie will need to walk to achieve her goal. However, there will be surrogates within the narrative who take on this mantle throughout the piece.

- The path: Help the little girl who is playing with Barbie in the real world.
- Off the path: Barbie's delusion that the world is a perfect place if everything were to stay the same.
- The wolf: The patriarchy … Interestingly, although this affects Barbie, and she must confront it at various points within the narrative, it is Ken who is both the representative of it at times and then defeats it when he goes on his own journey of sorts. He is almost an unknowing chosen one in his own subplot within the piece.
- The key: Barbie's belief that she can change the world in positive ways.
- The gate: the border between Barbie Land and the real world.
- The suit of armour: stereotypical Barbie's femininity … potentially with a side of post-feminism.

Act 2: Goodbye perfect world; hello patriarchy

Ken has a talk with another Ken, who insists that Barbie asked him to go with her, but he turned her down. A plan is forming in his mind that he is going to try and go with Barbie to the real world. Barbie then suggests that she is trying to find reasons to stay, but that she has to complete her mission. Her reluctance to continue is clearly to the fore here, as it should be with all unable-to-believe chosen ones. She is already asking herself the central question of this paradigm: 'Who am I meant to be?'

As she leaves, the other Barbies suggest that Barbie will be able to see all the good work that she has done in the real world and how much of a hero she will be out there. This whole exchange has the twinge of delicious irony to it that continues throughout the piece.

As Barbie heads away from Barbie Land in her car, she discovers that Ken has enacted his plan and stowed away. He then convinces Barbie that she will need him if there is 'beach', as he is a professional in it. They then make their way to the real world through various modes of transport before arriving on the rollerblades at the real beach. Here Barbie and Ken are stared at and mocked. Barbie admits to feeling self-conscious and that there is an undercurrent of threat to the looks that she is getting. She is now beginning to understand the differences between her once upon a time in Barbie Land and the threat(s) that she will face within the dark forest. Ken then explicitly states that it appears that everything has been 'reversed here' – a clear indication that they are in a new terrifying physical space that they will have to try and understand.

The pair then physically change their appearance. However, they end up wearing an equally interesting ensemble as the ones that they had on when they first arrived, choosing to wear cowgirl and cowboy costumes. They are unable to move beyond who they were in the first act as they have not grown or changed (yet), and the 'Who am I meant to be?' question is still very clearly being explored here.

Barbie and Ken then separate, with Barbie needing space to think about what she needs to do next. On his own, Ken begins to see the world is a place that allows him to embrace his masculinity, and he will be able to take charge of his own destiny away from Barbie with all the fist-pumping, high-fives and finance that he can get his hands on.

Meanwhile, Barbie has a reflective moment alone on a bench and begins to see flashes of the little girl who used to play with her. However, some of the later elements of the montage showcase that the child now has a broken relationship with her mother. This brings a tear to Barbie's eye, something that she admits is a new physical experience for her. Although she does also learn that the child she is looking for goes to Davy Crockett Junior High School, the next stop on her journey.

Glancing to her side, Barbie sees there is an old woman at the other end of the bench. Barbie then tells her how beautiful she is, and the pair share a laugh. It is a beat that doesn't really advance the plot of the piece and ultimately goes nowhere within the narrative. Allegedly it was a part of the film that was going to be cut early in the editing process; however, Gerwig told *Dateline*, 'If I cut the scene, I don't know what this movie is about.' Although as a creative you should always stick to your vision, remember that Gerwig is an established force in Hollywood and has much more clout than a first-time writer to ensure that elements like this stay in the pictures she makes. Ken returns excited about how men rule the world in the real world. Meanwhile, Barbie now knows that her child is at school. The pair are back on the path and ready for the next hurdle that they face.

We are then shown an extended sequence at Mattel where the FBI contacts the corporation to let them know that Barbie and Ken have escaped from Barbie Land. This also gives us a glimpse of Gloria who is currently drawing several macabre versions of Barbie as she looks after the reception desk. These will come more to the forefront of the narrative later; they are breadcrumbs for us to follow that are carefully placed so as not to appear contrived when they are of narrative importance.

Word of Barbie's and Ken's escape travels to the Board of Mattel which causes the CEO to nearly pass out. He worries that if word gets out about this it would be bad for the company. Gloria listens at the door and is also shocked by this revelation.

Act 3 (Part 1): Making women feel bad about themselves

Barbie and Ken arrive at the high school where they believe they will find the girl who should be playing with Barbie. Barbie admits to feeling anxious while Ken believes that he feels great. They are beginning to interrogate their emotional response to the new information they are learning about the world and themselves. The pair separate again, with Ken heading to the library to look for books on trucks while Barbie continues her mission on the path.

Barbie sees the young girl, called Sasha, who she believes is the one who is playing with her. However, before she heads over to confront her, she is advised by another student that she shouldn't do that as she will be crushed by her. Ignoring the advice, Barbie heads on over, hoping that she will receive a warm reception. She does not and discovers that the girls she is talking to have a somewhat negative perception of Barbie. It is evident that Sasha is the ringleader of these mean girls who goes as far to state that Barbie has 'been making women feel bad about themselves since [she] was invented'. Although Barbie protests, Sasha continues to pile in on her. This makes Barbie cry, and she runs away. The path is too hard to follow, and Barbie retreats to off the path where it is safe for her.

Ken, meanwhile, begins checking out the books that he can find about the patriarchy. He then goes to try and find himself a position that is worthy of his new-found supposed status. Ken attempts to get himself a job as an investment banker and then a doctor and then a lifeguard; however, he finds that he is not qualified for any of these roles. Ken then vows to go somewhere where he can start the patriarchy, fresh in his own image. Sat off the path, Barbie is still bereft about her recent revelation. She doesn't get long to wallow in her pity, however, as Mattel kidnaps her.

Gloria picks Sasha up from school, and her daughter alerts her to the fact that, earlier on, she saw a woman who believed she was Barbie. Gloria puts two and two together and understands that this is the real Barbie who has been sent from Barbie Land.

Barbie arrives at the Mattel offices where the CEO suggests that if Barbie were to simply 'get into the box' then everything would be OK – an interesting metaphorical device that both would signal a literal stasis for our chosen one (she would be strapped into a prison of sorts) and also something of a thematic exploration in that it would define Barbie in a box as simply a stereotype. Mattel would be able to forever keep Barbie off the path by force, everything would stay the same, and Barbie would not be able to experience her become-a-swan moment.

Barbie harmlessly asks to see 'the women in charge' and is disappointed when she is told that the entire board is filled with men. She does get into the box, but before the zip ties can close around her wrists, Barbie moves her hands and asks if she can go to the restroom. She then escapes and runs through the building. The Board of Mattel give chase, but Barbie is able to give them the slip. She then arrives in a long corridor, where she meets her creator, Ruth, with whom she has a conversation about looking perfect. She confesses that the real world isn't what she thought it was, to which her creator responds, 'It never is. And isn't that marvellous?'

After getting further directions from Ruth, Barbie is able to escape. She has begun to understand that in order to make the world a better place (fulfil her want), she is going to have to readjust her belief that everything has to stay the same. Ruth is one of the mentor figures who takes on some of the mechanics of the role within the narrative. This is appropriate for the woman who literally made Barbie and further helps with the exploration of the repeated question, 'Who am I meant to be?'

Gloria then pulls up outside the building and instructs Barbie to get into the car.

Midpoint: 'Come jump in'

During the ensuing car chase, Gloria admits that she is the one who has been playing with Barbie recently, and that she has made Barbie sad like her with thoughts of death and cellulite. Barbie realizes that she has not come into the real world to help Sasha but is actually there to help Gloria. The memories she saw in the beginning were not Sasha's but Gloria's. We then see a montage outlining this. Barbie confesses that she thought that Barbie had made the world a better place, but now she sees that it is forever and irrevocably messed up. The three in the car then have a thematic discussion about the role of women in a world that has not been shaped in their image.

Gloria then showcases a particular skill for evasive driving and gives the Mattel Corp drivers the slip. Barbie then takes Gloria and Sasha back to Barbie Land, reversing the journey that she initially took with Ken. As they go through the steps to get to Barbie Land, Barbie outlines what Gloria and Sasha should expect from Barbie Land and how it will be entirely run by women. This is the representation of her easy plan.

Act 3 (Part 2): 'Hiya, Barbie!'

The Board of Mattel recognize that Barbie has taken Gloria and Sasha to Barbie Land and immediately try and follow them there.

Arriving at Barbie Land, Barbie thinks that in bringing Gloria to Barbie Land she has done everything that she will need to do in order to 'fix' herself and her once upon a time, even saying that she can 'feel her heels lifting already'. However, she discovers that Barbie Land has changed in her absence after Ken bought back the knowledge of patriarchy, and the various Barbies she left behind are now subservient to the Kens.

Getting back to her Dreamhouse, Barbie sees that Ken has taken over and remodelled her place in his image, calling it his Mojo Dojo Casa House.

Back in the real world, as the Board of Mattel being rollerblading towards Barbie Land, they discover that Ken has also had an impact on reality with the toy sets of his Mojo Dojo Casa House flying off the shelves. Both worlds are being affected by the decisions that Barbie has made. Back in Barbie Land, Ken delivers an emotional speech about how he now feels like someone and how Barbie has failed him because he previously has felt so worthless. It appears that Ken has one last plan which is to call a special election to make Ken the president of the now renamed Kendom and change the constitution. Ken then kicks Barbie out of her own house so he can start a 'boy's night'.

Barbie is bereft as Ken throws out what remains of her clothes. She then monologues about how she was perfect before Gloria infected her with human thoughts and emotions. Sasha jumps to her mother's defence saying that it was actually all Barbie's fault that this happened. Barbie retorts that she has never wanted anything to change (again conservative in her estimations of the world). Gloria replies that's just how life is. Here she more forcefully takes on the role of a surrogate mentor figure of sorts, trying to get her chosen one to see how she needs to grow and develop in this terrifying dark forest that she is venturing through.

However, Barbie rejects it and tries to remove herself from the path further still. Sat down on the ground, she hopes that 'one of the more leadership-orientated Barbies sorts out this whole mess'. She insists that she just wants to give up and says that Gloria and Sasha should simply go home. She then says, 'This is the lowest that I have ever been emotionally and physically'. This is great line for outlining where we are at within the narrative structure of the piece. We then are shown an advert for 'Depression Barbie' before Weird Barbie gets our Barbie, who is still on the floor, to snap out of her current state and starts to drag her back onto the path.

On the way out of Barbie Land, Gloria and Sasha find that Alan has smuggled himself into the back of their car. He tells them about the plan that the Kens have to separate the real world and the Kendom by building a large wall between them, something they are currently not very adept at. Alan then fights with the Construction Kens before Sasha tells Gloria that they have to go back and save Barbie Land. Sasha implores her mother to go back to save Barbie Land because, 'You've always believed in what she could be', and saying further, 'Even if you can't make it perfect you can make it better.' She then reveals that she has always liked her drawings that are weird and dark and crazy – things that she admires in her mother.

Once Alan returns to the car, Gloria and Sasha decide that they are going to return to Barbie Land to make things right again. Alan laments that he will never be able to get out of here.

Act 4: Saved by monologuing

Arriving at Weird Barbie's house, we see that she is in the process of trying to deprogramme the Barbies who have been most affected by the transition to a Kendom. The process is not going well; however, the brainwashing has not worked on stereotypical Barbie, and she simply lies on the floor continuing to be depressed and refusing to move back onto the path. It appears that she thinks that you are either brainwashed or weird and ugly – none of the things that she wants.

Gloria, Sasha and Alan arrive. Gloria tries to get Barbie to believe in herself after she has had a dramatic crisis in confidence. She then launches into a monologue that is not only about getting Barbie back up on her feet but that also explores the central thematic idea of the role modern women play in society and the cognitive dissonance that is required to be a woman under the patriarchy. In doing this, she gets one of the brainwashed Barbies to become herself again, and then Barbie hatches a plan to get Gloria to explain this to the other brainwashed Barbies after extracting them from the influence of their Kens by using the patriarchy against them.

Although this would more typically be delivered by the mentor figure (Weird Barbie), it makes sense within the broader context of the film that this should be Gloria's monologue. However, this, and the ensuing plan to right the wrongs of the world, are all done under the watchful eye of Weird Barbie. The plan goes exactly as expected, and Gloria is able to deprogramme the rest of the Barbies with a continuation of her monologue.

The final stage of the plan is to get the original Ken to admit his misdeeds and have stereotypical Barbie confront him head on at his Mojo Dojo Casa House. As Ken plays his guitar at Barbie in his house, we then transition to the beach where he and the various other Kens are 'serenading' their respective Barbies. During this, the Barbies sow discord amongst the Kens by flirting with the other versions of them in front of them, wounding their egos and getting them to turn on one another. The Kens then decide to go to war against the other Kens within the Kendom. (We told you that this might get a little confusing …)

Ken then has a revelation of his own through his performance of (the Oscar-nominated) song 'I'm Just Ken' as he and his namesakes first physically fight and then dance off. However, despite his psychological growth, the plan that the Barbies have come up with has worked, and they are able to change the constitution back to what it used to be. The Kens arrive back at their houses to realize that their Mojo Dojo Casa Houses have reverted back to Dreamhouses.

Barbie and Ken then have a heart-to-heart in her bedroom where it is clear that Ken doesn't actually want to be in charge. Barbie then tells Ken that he has to discover who he really is without her. Likewise, she has to uncover who she is without him.

The CEO of Mattel arrives and thanks the Barbies for helping him too. President Barbie then begins to assist in making Barbie Land a little more equal for the Kens and rewarding Weird Barbie for her work during the narrative of the film.

Gloria then approaches the CEO of Mattel and asks him if they could create an 'Ordinary Barbie'. He initially rejects it as a terrible idea until he is told that it will make them money. As he is about to close the portal between the two worlds, Sasha asks, 'What about Barbie?' He insists that the most logical ending is that she is in love with Ken. However, this isn't the ending that we have been working towards, and it is time for her to fully reveal herself as having been a swan this whole time.

Ruth arrives from behind everyone and finally announces herself as the inventor of Barbie. She invites Barbie to walk with her, and the pair wander into the distance as the rest of Barbie Land wave them off.

Last throw of the dice: 'I can't give you permission'

In a pastel void, Ruth outlines all of the good work that Barbie has done during the narrative. Self-effacing to the end, Barbie doesn't take credit but rather shares it, answering, for herself, the question 'Who am I meant to be?' Ruth then outlines that Barbie is able to become a human but would have to experience what it means to be one in its totality, accepting the beauty and the pain that will come with it. She also deconstructs the symbolism that Barbie represents within the semiotic order (the postmodernism during this final act really begins to ramp up here).

Ruth then lets her know that Barbie doesn't have to ask permission to become human, that power has been inside her this whole time. She tops it all off with the line, 'We mothers stand still so our daughters can look back to see how far they have come', reinforcing her status of a mentor figure within the piece. Barbie accepts Ruth's hands which allows her to see what it truly means to be human through a series of home videos showing a range of women experiencing their lives. Ruth leaves her as she finally accepts this and spiritually transforms.

Act 5: If the shoe fits

Now in the real world, Barbie heads to have a gynaecological exam proudly wearing her Birkenstock sandals.

10

Accidental case study
Everything Everywhere All at Once (2022)

Logline: An unhappy wife and mother is forced to confront her own shortcomings in a fantastical trip through the multiverse.
Release date: 13 May 2022
Screenplay: Daniel Kwan and Daniel Scheinert

As an extended metaphor into familial relationships which doesn't get boring, *Everything Everywhere All at Once* takes some beating. Despite the apparent complexity of the film, at heart this is a simple tale of growing understanding between mother, daughter and husband with the added dimension of parallel universes. Parallel universes have been familiar devices in films ever since screenwriters were able to digest Gabriele Veneziano's concept of string theory, which he came up with back in the late 1960s. It took about twenty years for Robert Zemeckis and Bob Gale to really get their heads around it with *Back to the Future*, and since then the parallel universe gates have been flung wide, embraced wholeheartedly by Christopher Nolan in his sci-fi, wormhole, future-of-the-human-race epic, *Interstellar* (2014); his sci-fi, dream-travelling thriller, *Inception* (2010); and his sci-fi, backwards-time-travel actioner, *Tenet* (2020), and also familiar from across the genres in films such as *Groundhog Day* (1993), in which disgruntled weatherman Phil Connors is forced to live the same day over and over; *Terminator* (1984), in which a cyborg from the future is sent back in time to change history; *The Matrix* (1999), in which Neo is shown that humankind has been enslaved by intelligent machines; and the Marvel franchise (2008 to present) over the course of which time is bent every which way. Even Harry Potter experiences a parallel time slip in *Harry Potter and the Prisoner of Azkaban* (2004) when he and Hermione go back three hours in time to free Sirius Black from the Dementors.

Arguably, *Everything Everywhere All at Once* takes the scientific thesis to its ultimate endpoint in popular film-making, but there is probably a popular film-maker out there about to prove us wrong.

Act 1: 'Every day here is a battle'

The story begins, as most well-written films on this pathway do, in a place of familiarity to our chosen one, but a place that is in need of improvement. We don't very often see prologues or cold opens on the accidental pathway, but, instead, the opening scenes must work hard to set up a once upon a time and a chosen one which are simultaneously comfortable yet flawed. While they will yearn to return home during their time in the dark forest, the accidental chosen one's once upon a time is often an unhappy or unfulfilling place. In *Back to the Future*, Marty McFly's family is dysfunctional; in *Die Hard*, John McClane's family is broken; in *Groundhog Day*, Phil Connors is a cynical, loveless weatherman. The once upon a time in these stories will begin to set up that which must be fixed by the story to come.

Thus, in *Everything Everywhere All at Once*, we meet Evelyn Wang and her husband Waymond, wrestling with tax receipts preparing for an audit into their chaotic laundromat business and getting ready for a Chinese New Year party to be attended by Evelyn's father, Gong Gong, all at the same time. Meanwhile, Waymond clutches divorce papers, and daughter Joy arrives with her girlfriend, Becky. There is a clear tension between Evelyn and Joy, particularly regarding her relationship with another woman – something Evelyn is determined not to tell Gong Gong. Joy is bitter.

This is a deliberately busy, chaotic, whirlwind of an opening, but it also gives us a good deal of information about the story to come. At the centre of the maelstrom is the chosen one, Evelyn, who is exhausted, unhappy and under pressure. As an example of a tightly written, information laden, seemingly complex yet deceptively simple opening, you would do well to look to the opening scenes of *Everything Everywhere All at Once*. There isn't a word wasted or an image out of place here. These writers know where they are going and why they are going there.

And so, the writers prepare us for the arrival of the second act as the intertitle 'EVERYTHING' appears on screen. We have already received a hint that all in Evelyn's life is not as it should be as we spy Waymond acting strangely in the laundromat, but the moment passes without comment. The true break into Act 2 happens as Evelyn stands in the lift on the way to meet the auditor.

Act 2: 'If I have to think about one more thing today, my head will explode'

As the lift heads towards their fateful meeting, Waymond is replaced by Alpha Waymond, Evelyn is fitted with her earpieces, and the dark forest looms. At this point, we are treated to a mini-montage of Evelyn's life to this date, and everything is … disappointing. Gong Gong's disappointment at her being a girl at birth; her parents' disappointment at Evelyn's desire to marry Waymond; Evelyn's disappointment at the laundromat; the deteriorating relationship between Evelyn and Joy; her father's deterioration in health … As a high-speed overview of Evelyn's life to this point, this is effective, simple, characterful storytelling. In a little over a minute, we have been provided with enough information to tell us that there is a situation that needs fixing here.

Given a number of seemingly meaningless tasks by Alpha Waymond, the family are confronted by fearsome auditor, Deirdre Beaubeirdre. Here, once again, we learn of Evelyn's frustrations with her life as Deirdre lists her business expenses for attempts to be a singer, a novelist, a chef, a teacher, a singing coach and so on. Twenty minutes into the film and Evelyn is given a glimpse of her life as the accidental chosen one when, following Waymond's bizarre instructions, she finds herself in the stationery cupboard, where she receives some garbled exposition about her importance in the story, but it is a few minutes later, at the thirty-minute point of the film, where the archetypal accidental invitation moment occurs.

The invitation: 'You are very bad at explaining'

Accidental chosen ones generally do not receive an invitation; they simply stumble into the dark forest. But here Alpha Waymond explicitly tells Evelyn, 'You can either come with me and live up to your ultimate potential, or lie here and live with the consequences.' Crucially, Evelyn opts to lie there and live with the consequences. However, Alpha Waymond physically lifts her up and carries her into the dark forest against her will. As with all accidental chosen ones, Evelyn does not choose to participate in the film. She, in fact, deliberately and definitively rejects the invitation.

We are thrust into the confusing madness of the dark forest at the same moment as Evelyn. Here Jobu Tupaki, the character who we will consider as the wolf for much of the story, is introduced immediately, but we would be well advised to remember that accidental narratives often do not have wolves … especially when Jobu Tupaki is revealed to be none other than Joy. Or at least a version of Joy.

It is a general rule of the accidental dark forest that the chosen one does not understand, first what they are doing there and second what are the rules that govern it. *Everything Everywhere All at Once* is a fairly extreme example of this in that the film-makers throw us immediately into the deep end with little in the way of solid information to go on. They are able to sustain audience buy-in at this point because we are already invested in the life of Evelyn and her family. There is a human story going on here as Deirdre struggles to get them to pay attention to the audit, Waymond struggles with the delivery of the divorce papers, Gong Gong struggles with his disappointment in his daughter, and Joy struggles with her own position in the family and her relationship with her mother.

The film neatly retains the once upon a time of the story throughout so that, while we are following Evelyn's wild adventures in the multiverse, we are also thoroughly grounded in the ongoing tale of the audit, the divorce, the family and Gong Gong's disappointment, but the all-important question that the accidental chosen one always asks themselves when on this pathway is clearly to the fore: 'Why am I here?'

In another frantic series of scenes in which Alpha Waymond provides us with more exposition but, as Evelyn points out, he is 'very bad at explaining', we are introduced to the key concept of 'verse jumping', which forms the basis of the journey that Evelyn is about to embark upon. Verse jumping allows characters to travel from one parallel universe to another. Despite the high-octane craziness of the narrative as it moves forward, this is a relatively simple concept which is easy for us, and for Evelyn, to grasp, with the extra added fun that alternative universes can only be accessed through the traveller using the 'Stochastic Path Algorhithm'. Basically, she has to enact a statistically improbable action to make a verse jump.

The very nature of accidental narratives means that they will often require exposition in order for us to fully understand what is going on and how to exit the dark forest. Either, as in *Back to the Future* or *Groundhog Day*, the chosen one will embark upon their own voyage of discovery, and we, as an audience, will experience the dark forest in tandem with them, or, as in *Soul* (2021) or *Labyrinth* (1986), a character or characters will explain the rules to the chosen one and we will learn them at the same time. It is important, in this storytelling, that, at least at the point of entry into the dark forest, we are standing alongside the chosen one, learning what they learn, experiencing what they experience so that, with them, we can figure out the way to get home. While *Everything Everywhere All at Once* does not shy away from exposition the writers provide something of a masterclass here in delivering complex information in a palatable way through fun and engaging storytelling. Once again, they are keeping the essential story simple by reminding us of the key stakes for Evelyn.

At this point in the story, the path is unclear. Our chosen one is still trying to work out why they are in this place. Dorothy had a Yellow Brick Road to guide her to the Emerald City, but, as we know, the Yellow Brick Road did not turn out to lead her directly to the gate that would help her exit the dark forest. For most of our accidental chosen ones, the path is not yet clear. They need to understand where they are first and 'Why am I here?' second. That second question generally takes quite a long time to answer.

After some near fatal difficulties in pulling off her first jump, during which time Alpha Waymond decides that she is not the Evelyn who will defeat Jobu Tupaki and heads off in search of another, Evelyn manages her jump and is not only transformed into a kung fu master but is also able to witness her life as it would have been had she not married Waymond, and that life is good. The realization that Evelyn's parallel lives may be better than her current one opens up an immediate danger for her but also leads to the story of what happened to Jobu. She verse-jumped too many times, and her mind became overloaded, fracturing and creating a being who lives in multiple universes simultaneously. Following her jump, Alpha Waymond is now convinced that this is the Evelyn who can defeat Jobu, warns her to take care when verse-jumping as it can damage the mind, potentially cracking 'like a clay pot holding water'.

Evelyn's path is clear now. She has been tasked with defeating Jobu Tupaki, who, in her own universe, is also her daughter. Naturally, Evelyn is going to be torn about this task and the path ahead, but events move so quickly in the world of this film so that we, and she, are not allowed the time to consider this existential dilemma before Jobu confronts Evelyn for the first time.

It is usual in the accidental narrative that requires this level of exposition that the path should only be revealed gradually, and here, almost an hour into a film that lasts around two hours and twenty minutes, is the point at which a clear route through the story for Evelyn is made clear. Interest is maintained here by constant innovation in the writing and film-making and the creation of strong characters for us to invest in, but this kind of craziness can only sustain the narrative for so long. Evelyn, and we, need to understand where the route through this dark forest is, otherwise we are simply watching events unfold rather than emotionally investing in them. As we enter Act 3, then, Evelyn is able to witness at first hand the character who appears to be the wolf in the story and to recognize the scale of the problem that lies before her in her attempts to return to a semblance of normality.

The core elements of the narrative moving forward, then, are:

- The path: Evelyn is tasked with defeating Jobu Tupaki if ever she is to return to her once upon a time.
- Off the path: Evelyn must experiment with the multiverse in order to achieve her aim, and herein lies the danger that she may never find her way out.
- The wolf: apparently, Jobu Tupaki … but accidental storylines don't generally need wolves.
- The suit of armour: Evelyn apparently has no suit of armour, but she will find that this is not the case.
- The key: Evelyn's realization that she actually loves her family.
- The gate: Evelyn's ability to manipulate the multiverse in a positive way.

Act 3 (Part 1): 'Nothing matters'

When Jobu arrives, we, and Evelyn, are treated to a display of her powers as she manipulates reality, but more important than Jobu's pyrotechnics and mind-bending theatrics is Evelyn's reaction to her, as Evelyn accuses Jobu of being the reason Joy doesn't call her, why she dropped out of college, why she has tattoos and why she 'thinks she's gay'. Despite all of the madness and complexity of the world of *Everything Everywhere All at Once*, at this point, nearing the midpoint of the film, we are made to understand that the whole story is essentially about the mother–daughter relationship.

However, it is also a film about the manipulation of every aspect of the physical world as seen through the prism of the multiverse, so when Jobu tells Evelyn that she has placed everything on a bagel and that is emblematic of her belief that 'nothing matters', in this film it makes perfect sense.

The concept of rising action in the accidental narrative works somewhat differently to other story pathways due to the helplessness of the chosen one in this alien space. They have entered the world of the story with no discernible suit of armour, and therefore the first half of the journey through the dark forest is often a version of falling action in which the chosen one continues to fail in their efforts to understand the dark forest and find a way to leave it. In most narratives, as they enter the dark forest, the chosen one will see clearly the route in front of them whether they want to be there or not. On the accidental pathway, the chosen one is initially powerless and in the control of the dark forest. The second half of the journey, following the midpoint, will be the section of their journey where they will begin to fight back … off the path.

Midpoint: 'Just like her'

When Evelyn is saved by Alpha Gong Gong, she is provided with the final piece of exposition that will eventually enable her to recognize the Gate which will help her to exit the dark forest: Alpha Waymond tells her that, in this universe, she is the worst version of herself. So many unrealized dreams and unfinished goals means that this Evelyn is capable of anything because she is so bad at everything. The final piece of the puzzle, in this extended midpoint, falls into place when Alpha Gong Gong tells Evelyn to kill her daughter so that Jobu will have one less version of herself to access.

This is the moment of choice for Evelyn where she finally grasps a way to return the world to a semblance of her once upon a time. She decides not to kill Joy, but instead she determines to save her daughter by becoming 'just like her' and embracing every aspect of the multiverse. This moment, by the way, in a seemingly chaotic, anarchic film, is at the mathematical midpoint: one hour and ten minutes into a film lasting two hours and twenty minutes.

Despite all appearances, this is a carefully constructed screenplay based upon well-established screenwriting principles. The key moments of discovery clustered around this point in the story reveal new information to Evelyn and alter the trajectory of the story. As with most powerful midpoints, this is, initially at least, a downward trajectory as Alpha Gong Gong calls upon every alpha jumper to congregate on their location in order to stop Evelyn in her plans; however, in broad storytelling terms, this point represents a rising trajectory for Evelyn as she begins to put her failures behind her and forge her own way, off the path, through the dark forest towards the gate.

Act 3 (Part 2): 'There is always something to love'

There follows a spectacular action sequence in which Evelyn accesses random alternate versions of herself in order to defeat the army of alpha jumpers ranged against her. The battle is completed following a stand-off with Alpha Gong Gong and the endorsement of Alpha Waymond who recognizes that her plan might actually work, despite managing 'to piss off everyone in the multiverse'. In his universe, however, Alpha Waymond is attacked by Jobu, and he loses his life. Evelyn confronts Jobu and announces that she will defeat her, as she is reaching her full potential. Then Evelyn dies, and the film comes to an end.

In an imaginative, anarchic film, this moment, even two-thirds of the way through the film, provides a big surprise after over an hour of constant surprises. In effect, this moment, manipulated by Jobu, represents the intervention of the gatekeeper. Just as it looks as if Evelyn has understood her role in the story and is heading towards defeating Jobu and returning stability to the universes, the gate disappears. Jobu has the power to entirely stop the forward momentum of the story and send Evelyn back into the darkest reaches of the dark forest because Evelyn still has something to learn.

So, even though Evelyn is not dead, she finds herself running loose through the multiverse, and it starts to affect her grip on 'reality', just as it affected Jobu. The question here is will Evelyn go down the same path as her daughter and conclude that nothing matters? Or will she actually be able to save Joy and return to a semblance of her once upon a time? This is a subset, of course, of Evelyn's larger overarching question, 'Why am I here?'

The intervention of the gatekeeper is absolutely central to the design of an effective accidental narrative. The journey through the accidental dark forest is one of learning, understanding and growth. Initially, the chosen one is learning about the world they have entered; second, they must begin to understand why they are there and how they are able to leave; and, last, the most difficult step for them is growth. The story began in a flawed place. Something was wrong with the chosen one and the once upon a time that they inhabited, and, without this last element of growth, no real change will have been effected through the narrative. The chosen one needs a gatekeeper to send them back because they have still not recognized what it is within themselves that needs fixing, and this will be the whole point of the story.

Everything Everywhere All at Once is, at heart, a story about a mother and a daughter, and at this point Evelyn is still talking about defeating Jobu. Still to come is her realization that, even though she did not enter with a suit of armour, she does carry the key, within herself, that will open the gate. Also, remember, accidental dark forests rarely contain wolves. So, perhaps Jobu isn't the wolf after all …

Battling with her own persona in an increasingly fast-paced trip through the multiverse, just as Evelyn appears to have lost her grip on reality altogether and the worlds of the multiverse proliferate at an ever-increasing, mind-bending speed, it all stops. Evelyn has won the battle with the chaos in her head, and the next intertitle appears with 'PART TWO: EVERYWHERE' on screen.

Act 4: A random rearrangement of particles

In the five-act structure, what the film-makers call Part Two is actually the break into Act 4 where the chosen one must dig deep in order to realize what it is that is continuing to tether them to the accidental dark forest and allow them to move into the final act of the story. In the world of *Everything Everywhere All at Once*, this is, indeed, the second part of Evelyn's journey as she has gained control over the multiverse and is, from this point, able to manipulate the world just as Jobu can.

The central dramatic question of whether her control will lead her down the same path as Jobu remains as Jobu reveals to Evelyn her perspective on reality as she and Evelyn move from universe to universe, ridiculous scenario to ridiculous scenario, ending in a rather weak physical fight in which Evelyn vows to defeat Jobu. Even the attempt at physical combat here shows us that, despite her control over the very particles that make up the multiverse, Evelyn has still not grasped how she can exit the dark forest.

Alpha Waymond, from a different universe to the other Alpha Waymond (stick with it), tells Evelyn, during this whistle-stop tour of alternate existences, that all of this chaos is Evelyn's fault. She, or a version of her, invented verse-jumping and thereby created Jobu Tupaki. Once again, the metaphorical mother–daughter relationship is brought to the fore, and the simplicity at the heart of the storytelling is revealed. Evelyn created Jobu just as Evelyn created Joy. However, this Alpha Waymond also points something out that will be vital in Evelyn's attempts to pass through the gate: there is no evil villain in this story, 'just a whole lot of confusing hubbub'. It is human beings' inability to be satisfied with their lot, or always looking for a better version of themselves, that has created the mess that feeds *Everything Everywhere All at Once*.

Here, then, is the key revealed that will unlock the gate. Evelyn is the source of all the disruption in the multiverse, just as she is the source of the disruption in her own home and family due to her dissatisfaction with her lot. There will be two phases to the way in which she works out how to exit this story: the first will be the way in which she opts to manipulate the particles of the universe; the second will be the simple realization of how she feels about herself and her family.

Finally, Evelyn is taken to a temple where all of Jobu's followers are gathered to praise the bagel – the bagel that they all wish to be sucked inside because, inside the bagel, there are no more beliefs, therefore no more conflict. At this moment of ridiculous, comic catharsis in which the ultimate expression of the multiverse is identified as a bread roll, the real message of the story is also revealed when Jobu tells Evelyn of the formative moment that affected Joy's transition into her: when she told her mother that she was gay, and Evelyn didn't respond. Evelyn just went on with her life, and Joy was deeply hurt. Evelyn ignored a revelation so important to Joy that it broke their relationship. These two moments are juxtaposed in this turning point in the story. The bagel and the fractured relationship. That one single moment in the relationship of a mother and daughter could bring about such cataclysmic consequences. Joy's belief that her great revelation to her mother meant nothing to her transformed her into Jobu and lead her to the conclusion that nothing in all the universes held any meaning. Once again, the wolf in the story is not Jobu but within Evelyn herself.

When Evelyn finally stares into the bagel, she is confronted by the meaningless of her life … the meaningless of all of her lives. As, once again, we cycle through Evelyn's various universes, this time she does her best to undermine each of them. She appears to be lost as she fails again and again in the multiverse, and Jobu looks on eagerly as Evelyn seems to be heading the same way as her but admitting that she wasn't looking for Evelyn so that they could fight but so that she could find somebody who could feel what she feels … everything everywhere all at once.

In the most familiar of the universes, the laundromat, Evelyn begins to smash the place up, telling everyone how much she hates it, asking herself for another, angst-ridden time, 'Why am I here?' She cycles faster and faster through the universes, seeing the negative in all of them. She sees what Jobu sees and understands … before becoming a rock.

Evelyn and Jobu are rocks together in a deserted landscape – a universe where life failed to form, which provides refuge for Jobu. They debate the pointlessness of existence and the futility of humanity for a moment … before they stand, once more, before the bagel. Jobu tries to persuade Evelyn to enter the bagel with her so that they can both die together.

The last throw of the dice: 'There's no place like home'

In the formulation of an accidental storyline, all of the narrative is focused around the moment at which the chosen one finally realizes how to get home because in this moment is the secret of why they are here, in this dark forest, in the first place: the answer to the 'Why am I here?' of the narrative. The accidental storyline often contains within it a strong moral or message for the audience, and strong morals and messages are generally very simple. In *The Wizard of Oz*, Dorothy realizes, right at the end of the film, that she had the ruby slippers on her feet all the time and that there is 'no place like home'. In the case of *Everything Everywhere All at Once*, Evelyn has lost her way. She has forgotten that her love for her husband and daughter override all of the other dissatisfactions in her life. In this moment, she is reminded of this simple truth that she has carried with her throughout the story just as Dorothy has worn the ruby slippers.

As the bagel looms before her, Evelyn is pulled back to 'reality' by her husband, Waymond, who she finally sees in a new light. Waymond is a good man, fighting for his family and wanting people to be nice to one another. Jobu still tries to persuade Evelyn to enter the bagel where she will not have to deal with the mess of the multiverse, but, instead, Evelyn hugs Waymond in the laundromat as she realizes that she is in love with him.

Act 5: 'Evelyn, please, no more fighting'

Jobu is annoyed that Evelyn seems to have found meaning in her life and gathers all of her forces together to enter the bagel as Waymond begs, 'Evelyn, please, no more fighting.' Evelyn's life is threatened, but she finds a way out. Once again, cycling through the multiverse, this time she sees hope and positivity rather than meaninglessness, and the question of whether or not Evelyn will go down the same path as Jobu is answered. As the forces of Jobu and the alphas are massed against her, Evelyn uses the same techniques as Jobu in manipulating the very fabric of existence, but this time for good. Grenades turn into perfume spray, deadly enemies kiss … Evelyn instinctively knows and understands the weaknesses, desires and hopes of the enemies ranged against her, and she is able to make them come to pass but in a positive way.

Her final confrontation is with Alpha Gong Gong who is angry with her at her manipulation of the universe, but she turns on him and asks him why he could let her go as a child. Another trauma rises to the surface as Evelyn puts herself back together again. She is beginning to realize that she is okay and that, as a result, the daughter who reminds her so much of herself, is okay too.

Finally, Jobu attacks Evelyn physically, but each blow is deflected and turned into something beautiful, sweet, kind … But it isn't over yet as the final conflict between mother and daughter requires Evelyn to dig even deeper and to admit all of those things that she really feels about Joy but that, ultimately, she still wants to be with her. Despite everything, their love wins out. In every universe we have visited on Evelyn's journey, Waymond, Joy and Evelyn come together as a family.

Just before the film ends, we enter the final part of the story as the intertitles 'PART THREE: ALL AT ONCE' emerge. Joy puts her head on Evelyn's shoulder. Evelyn embraces Joy's girlfriend, Becky. Waymond and Evelyn kiss. They return to the tax office, where Deirdre continues to flick through their paperwork, but now they are united as a family, and their future promises to be happier together.

Everything Everywhere All at Once takes the audience on a highly imaginative and original journey, but its success as a piece of storytelling relies on the fact that it is a narrative grounded in simplicity of message and one that utilizes familiar and effective narrative tools to tell its tale. Evelyn enters the dark forest seemingly with no suit of armour, but deep within her is the love that will provide her with the key to open the gate. She sets off on a path through the dark forest and decides that she will be able to defeat Jobu by embracing the whole of the multiverse, but Jobu, the gatekeeper, returns her to the dark forest even when she has achieved this because Evelyn has yet to find the key. As with most accidental narratives, Evelyn is her own wolf. Jobu Tupaki is not a wolf at all. When constructing these narratives, remember that the core moment of self-discovery for the chosen one must come late on in the narrative, and this must contain a moment of self-realization that will see the once upon a time to which they return irrevocably changed.

11

Mistaken case study
Talk to Me (2023)

Logline: After discovering that she can conjure spirits with an embalmed hand, a grieving teenager unleashes a terrifying supernatural force.
Release: 27 July 2023
Screenwriters: Danny Philippou, Bill Hinzman, Daley Pearson

Talk to Me is a solid representation of the Mistaken arc. The piece has the vigour and energy of youth in its limbs and feels like an evolution of some of the more tired tropes within the canon of ghost and possession stories. This is particularly true of the film's use of social media and mobile phones, which are frequently used within the narrative both to document and to reinforce the theme of the importance of authentic vs simulated communication. Characters are often engaging with the world (or in some cases not engaging with the world) through the screens in their palms. They document the action of the seances and then watch back 'memories' of previous experiences. In a lesser narrative experience, this would be the only thematic idea driving the story; however, *Talk to Me* offers us much more than this.

The central *What if?* to the narrative is a simplistic one: what if seances were addictive? However, the work always ensures that character remains at the heart of the story with our chosen one, Mia, attempting to overcome her conflicted nature born out of grief. This allows for the inner and the outer journey of the narrative to directly reflect one another as Mia attempts to overcome her grief in an unhealthy way that will lead to her destruction.

The central 'sin' that must be a driving force behind all mistaken narratives is that of addiction and the genetic predisposition for being an addict. This fits neatly into the category of familial sin and allows for stories to explore the effects of generational trauma(s). The embalmed hand that is central to the conceit of the story becomes a metaphor for drug use/abuse as Mia slowly succumbs to 'using' it in order to see the spirit of her mother who died by suicide. Much like substances that offer some temporary comfort to those who use them and encourage continuous use, the entities seemingly deceive the user, offering them merely what they want to hear rather than what they need to hear. Again, this interesting distinction assists us as writers as it allows for a greater exploration of the central conflicted nature of the chosen one.

The true horror of *Talk to Me* comes when the path and off the path within the narrative collide and the insidious nature of the hand is fully revealed as the voices tell Mia to hurt the ones who love and care for her. How we reach out, through talking and physical contact, becomes a motif and a strong element of the visual storytelling of the piece. Mia has her surrogate family who is trying to help her heal, but she isn't fully allowing this to happen. 'Talk to me', it seems, is both a command for the person who is using the hand and a desire for connection. How it is that we reach out to loved ones whether they are no longer physically here or present but mentally elsewhere is the central thematic idea that drives the work and informs all of the other questions that are asked within the piece. This would include the different ways in which Mia answers the question, 'Who am I?', at the beginning and the end of the narrative.

Prologue: First-hand experience

We are introduced to the world of *Talk to Me* and the stakes for using the hand in the narrative. A young man (Cole) has locked himself in a room at a party and is evidently distressed. He has been using the hand frequently and is now experiencing some sort of psychotic breakdown. His brother (Duckett) arrives to collect him, and Cole stabs him before plunging the knife into his own head. This is a brilliant attention-grabbing opening sequence, clearly setting out the tone for the piece and establishing the core antagonism. It also gives us in the audience a clear indication of the intent of the narrative and delivers on the expectation of the genre (horror) settling us in with a solid set piece.

Act 1: Lend me a hand

We are introduced to Riley, who is so innocent that he won't even take a drag on an illicit cigarette. Mia arrives in her car and offers him a lift. It is clear that she is protective of the young man and to all intents and purpose part of his family. They hit a kangaroo on the way home. Mia drives off, leaving the animal in the middle of the road. When they arrive back at the house, Mia goes to speak to Jade. However, she engages with her phone rather than speak to the person in front of her. This clearly showcases the desire for connection that Mia has and how there are now a variety of things within the twenty-first century that are disrupting the opportunities to communicate in an authentic way.

Mia wants to go to the party where the hand is to 'see if it's real'. There is a short exchange that establishes that Mia potentially has feelings for Jade's current boyfriend – a foreshadowing of conflicts that are to come within the narrative. The entirety of this sequence sets up some of the larger conflicts that will run throughout the piece: What is reality and what is fiction (imagined)? What is spectacle and what is authenticity? What is it to be alone and what is it to be part of a community?

The pair eventually arrive at the party with Riley tagging along. Here it is clear that Mia is an outcast at the fringes of this group. Again, when she tries to chat with the people, she is met with the glazed look of someone on their phone. Hayley, one of the current owners of the possessed hand, even outright asks Jade at one point, 'Why did you bring her?'

The invitation: Talk to the hand

Mia volunteers to go first with the hand, replacing the young Riley believing that she will be a willing chosen one. This is a clear example of the classic hero being thrown into an adventure by taking the place of another. In our first book, we call this the take-me-instead moment, but little does Mia know that the action will begin her mistaken journey.

Hayley and Joss outline the rules for the hand, and they begin the ceremony, reiterating that if you follow the rules then everything will be fine. However, just like the farmer in 'The Goose that Laid the Golden Eggs', Mia will become greedy and seek to disobey the rules for her own gain. The pair that currently own the hand are the wolves of the narrative at this point. They oversee the dark forest, though it is clear that they are not going to be ready for the ensuing problems they will cause and actually behave out of misplaced bravado.

Mia uses the hand and lets the entity in so that it can take over her body. She has now broken the world and interrupted her identity. She begins the start of her physical transformation and starts to move into the dark forest and the question that all mistaken chosen ones ask themselves – 'What have I done?' – begins to resonate with her.

Act 2: I gotta hand it to ya

During her first possession, Mia singles out Riley for some of the more terrifying dialogue, telling him to 'Run!' over and over again. They are finally able to wrestle the hand off her and break the communication with the dead. However, Hayley mentions that they went a little over the allotted time that someone is able to keep hold of the hand, reinforcing the rules of the narrative and alerting us to the idea that Mia has now sinned and moved into the dark forest.

The mechanics of the piece are now set in motion:

- The path: This is to overcome grief. We will see that Mia is always chasing the hand.
- Off the path: This is Mia's interactions with the friends and surrogate family that could have helped her. This is particularly well represented by her interactions with Sue, Riley and Jade.
- Suit of armour: Mia is one of the mistaken chosen ones who is in a metaphorical swimsuit, as outlined in our chapter explicitly exploring the mechanics of a mistaken chosen one. Although she is on a journey

to take on the mantle of the wolf within this space, she is never able to fully realize that. She is happy experimenting with the hand but is unable to manage the fallout when it gets serious.

- The wolf: Mia begins to take on the mantle of the wolf. However, the central entity that stalks the dark forest is the real wolf that plagues the piece.
- The gate and the key: As it is with all mistaken narratives there is no gate or key that will assist in helping our chosen one. They will be trapped in the dark forest. In this instance, Mia will eventually become one of the entities trapped on the other side of the hand.

Back at the party, everyone celebrates, believing that this was the best possession they have experienced. We are then offered a brief image of an axolotl. These amphibians are known within the animal kingdom for being able to regenerate limbs when they are removed. A nod not only to the motif of the removed hand but also a possible nod to the momentous change that our chosen one is about to embark upon.

Returning to Jade's house, Jade now won't let Riley sleep in her room after being freaked out by what happened at the party. Mia is staying over on the couch and is okay with him crashing next to her. This again reinforces Mia's status as a protector.

Mia confesses to Riley about having nightmares. She worries about no longer existing and describes how when she looks into the mirror she doesn't see her reflection. This is another nice bit of foreshadowing. She explains how the hand has begun to change her physically, and it is clear that she will be going back to experience it again. This exchange also allows her to explore the feelings she has about the death of her mother and explain to the audience what happened to her. She explains that her mother died in the bathroom with her father trying to break down the door to reach her. Her description of her mother being 'on the other side' is interesting to have here as it holds within it plenty of subtext. After she confesses this to Riley, he says that Mia will always have him and Jade. This reinforces the found family that she has around her and also sets the stakes of the film now.

As the path and off the path begin to merge to the point where Mia is swallowed by the dark forest, she will increasingly expose those around her to danger. Mia then rather cryptically replies, 'It's OK. I don't feel alone anymore.' This possibly alerts us in the audience that she knows of the change that she is about to go through and the idea that the entitics have their grip on her. This exchange enhances the tone of the piece and allows for increased foreboding, with the thunderstorm in the background furthering assisting with this.

After a short sequence where there is a well-managed scare, we head to the school that the teenagers attend and see that Jade and Mia return to Hayley to ask to use the hand again almost as if they are arranging an illicit party. Following this scene, we are treated to a nice off-the-path sequence, where Riley and Jade's mum try to get the various teenagers in her house to confess to planning a party. However, none of them fall for it, and we see the close relationships that they all seem to share. We also learn that Mia has tried smoking weed once, showcasing how it is not her initial disposition to be attracted to drugs but that Jade's mother had potentially pegged her as the one most likely to cause trouble of the bunch.

This time, when the hand emerges, Daniel, Jade's boyfriend, tries using it. As he does, it appears that the spirit allows Daniel to express his repressed feelings about his girlfriend and has a rather intimate encounter with the family dog. During this section of the narrative, the rather ambiguous nature of the origins of the hand are explored. This is effective writing here as it helps to divert all questions an audience might have about the specifics of how the hand works. One of the golden rules of all great horror writing is never to over-explain the monster you have created as you can tie yourself up in knots. Once you have established the logic of the monster that you have created, just ensure that you stay true to its initial motivations. An audience can (and in most cases should) attribute greater meaning to the broader metaphor of the piece you have created. However, textually, the monster should be terrifying and want to destroy the harmony of the world you have created. Why it wants to do this should be linked to the initial sin of the piece but left ambiguous after that.

As Daniel leaves the room, feeling humiliated, Mia is desperate to have another go and straps herself in. We then get a montage where the cast all try using the hand in a carefree way with odd but fun interactions. Daniel will eventually return in order to get involved again (after they have put the dog outside).

Act 3 (Part 1): Don't bite the hand that feeds you

Now Riley wants to give the hand a go. His sister refuses; however, Mia convinces them to let him do it for a shorter amount of time than usual because he is too young to be experiencing an encounter with the entities. This is the most violent and disturbing encounter yet. Riley sees Mia's mother and then, as he is possessed by the entity, begins talking directly to Mia as her mother. Here the path and off the path have entirely collided, and Mia's desire to see her mother and the space off the path that she has previously been sheltered within are intertwined.

As it is with all Act 3s, we begin to experience the emotional investment from our chosen one in their journey through the dark forest and as they ask themselves the question 'What have I done?' Mia is obviously keen to hear more from her 'mother' and grasps Riley's hand tightly to the hand. She learns that there might be more to her mother's suicide, as it appears that she didn't mean to die, and that her father is keeping something from her. She is further breaking the rules demanding more time and refusing to let Riley the opportunity to remove himself from the ritual. She is slowly becoming more of the wolf. She is pushing for others to be a part of the ritual and breaking the rules when they are. She is starting to take charge of the dark forest.

Riley then begins slamming his head into the desk where he is sitting. Everyone is terrified. He continues to hold the hand and violently self-harms on various pieces of furniture in the house. Jade arrives and is mortified.

Everyone helps, except for Mia, who wanders out of the room looking strung out. Hayley and Joss say that they must get their story straight for when the police arrive. However, Mia then sees what she thinks is a flash of her mother at the door. It is clear that, despite everything that has happened, she is wanting to continue to follow the path she has set herself on no matter the consequences. She then heads to the sink and washes a huge amount of blood off her hands, not only advancing the motif of hands within the piece but also giving us an engaging moment of visual storytelling.

The pace of the narrative overtly begins to quicken here as Mia rapidly loses control of the situation. A great way to continue to ensure that your chosen one is being active and engaged within the narrative is to use a technique like this so that they are seemingly constantly trying to keep up with the world as it begins to change around them.

Midpoint: There's blood on your hands

The police arrive and quiz everyone. Mia's father then picks her up. When they are back home, she then confronts him in the kitchen about the death of her mother. There's something he isn't telling her. He doesn't respond. Mia heads into her room where she reveals that she has taken the hand. This again furthers her status as the wolf as she takes charge of the implement that has created this dark forest.

Meanwhile, at the hospital, Riley isn't in a good way. He's hooked up to machines with his mother and sister by his side. Mia heads to the hospital to see Riley, and it is clear that she isn't wanted there. Riley's mother simply asks Mia, 'Did you give him something?' She then tells Mia to go home. Mia experiences the warmth of the family diminishing and her returning to being an outsider in a space where she has previously only been welcomed. It is a further blow to her and a merging of the path and off the path.

Act 3 (Part 2): All hands to the pump

As she leaves, she sees a much clearer outline of her mother, who she follows into the bathroom. It is here that we begin to see that her addiction and dependence are progressing and the reality around her is collapsing. This externalization of these things is a great dramaturgical technique to showcase that our chosen one is getting more and more lost within the dark forest. We are then treated to a scare in the bathroom where she believes that her mother is trapped in the stall. She breaks down the door in a similar way to the brother in the prologue and presumably what her father did when discovering her mother. However, as Mia gets the door open, she finds out that no one is there.

She then talks to Daniel in the car as he drives her home from the hospital. She invites him back to hers as he cannot go home. He refuses because of the relationship that she has with Jade. However, she pushes him and says that she doesn't want to be alone. Is it that she is truly terrified of this? Or potentially is it that she has been emboldened by her experience in the dark forest and is attempting to manipulate him into coming back to her house? Both of these are interesting choices but not overtly delivered within the narrative.

Once they arrive at her house, Mia then tries to convince Daniel to use the hand with her. He refuses. Instead, they share memories of their early romance, and Daniel spies the declaration of love that he etched onto the furniture in her room. She is emboldened by her growing status as the wolf and is much more forward with him.

Daniel and Mia respectfully sleep head to toe. Mia watches videos of her mother on her phone – a twenty-first-century way of communicating with the dead. However, this is a simulation of communication and not what Mia actually wants. She then presses herself as close to Daniel as possible in order to feel his skin against hers, her desire for feeling the touch of another person achingly clear.

There's been a clap of thunder, and we're shown a dream sequence. We see Mia and Daniel kiss with the sound effects of someone trying to break the door down – the reality of Mia's mother's suicide. Mia then looks over Daniel's shoulder and sees her father attempting to revive her mother. She then wakes up from her dream/nightmare after looking at her hands all cut up and bloodied. From the corner of her room, an entity emerges and begins sucking Daniel's toes. He then wakes up to find that this is actually Mia who is doing this. Her reality is collapsing in on itself, and it is clear that she is in the grip of the power of the hand and unable to discern what is real and what isn't. Daniel leaves, a little disturbed with what has transpired, and Mia is left alone – something she has constantly professed to being terrified of. She freaks out, slapping herself and the furniture around her, clearly trying not to think about using the hand. However, she gets the implement out and sets up to use it on her own – an escalation of her addiction. As she opens her eyes, she sees what she believes to be her mother. She asks, 'Did you kill yourself?' The entity replies that she didn't, not on purpose. Mia is then told, in an incredibly sinister way, that Riley needs help. Mia lies down in bed with her mother who cradles her from behind in an embrace. Mia seemingly has got what she wanted.

Meanwhile, in the hospital, Riley's mother washes her badly damaged son with Jade. She gets a phone call and leaves Jade with him. He suddenly comes to bite his sister before smashing his head into the wall and then licking the blood off the floor. The entity, it seems, has more control over Riley than at first thought.

Act 4: It's all getting out of hand

Mia and the rest of the teenagers gather together to decide on a course of action and how they might be able to help Riley. Mia tentatively admits that she has been seeing stuff even without using the hand. She and Daniel have to come clean about how they slept in the same bed. This is something that Jade definitely disapproves of. This element is a slight pivot from the initial path where the want becomes to break the curse that Riley is under. This is smart writing as it allows for the narrative momentum to continue with an active protagonist who has something to move towards rather than being trapped in stasis. The breaking of a curse (as explained in the detailed chapter of the mistaken paradigm) is a great way to clearly establish a path that a chosen one is on and is a recognized and engaging mechanic to develop a narrative around.

We then hear about Duckett, and it is now revealed that he was the one who used the hand in the first place. This is the person who was stabbed in the prologue while trying to help his brother. When the group find Duckett, he isn't keen on helping them. Mia continues to follow him. She connects with him. He explains that his brother went too far. Interestingly, all of the language that is used here is of someone describing an addict. He says that the entities will get weaker the longer they are in him. However, it is clear that they are running out of time, and this isn't going to work for Riley.

Jade then explodes at Mia, both for what she has done to her brother and also for the betrayal that she feels about her actions with her boyfriend. The dark forest is collapsing around her, and there is nothing left for Mia as it really does seem that she is entirely alone. Jade even goes so far as saying that she wishes that Mia didn't force her way into her family. This is something that evidently stings and hits at a deep neurosis for Mia.

Mia suggests that they might not have blown out the candle that last time they did the ritual, which means that Riley might still be experiencing it: a possible way to break the connection with the other side and save Riley. Heading to the hospital, the group enacts the plan. The first time they try this, nothing happens. They then try to speak directly to Riley using the hand as a conduit. A little girl appears opposite Mia on the bed who promises to take her to where Riley is. The little girl shows Mia a terrifying space where Riley is being kept and tortured by a number of entities.

When Mia gets home, she is approached by her father who promises to be honest with her about the death of her mother. She sits down with him, and he reveals that her mother left her something before she died. It's a note. Her father reads it to her. From the note, it is clear that her mother wanted to die by suicide and her actions were her own and not an accident; however, the entity of her mother looms over her shoulder, saying it's not true and that her father is lying to her.

Mia then goes to her room where she discusses with the entity/her mother. During this discussion, Mia's mother/the entity says that Mia needs to go and kill Riley and that there is something terribly wrong with her father, who then seemingly breaks down the door and tries to kill her. However, this is a hallucination that Mia is having. As this is happening, her real father comes into the room just at the wrong moment, and, in her delusion, Mia stabs him in the neck with a pair of scissors. Mia then rings Jade, luring her away from Riley to her house so that she can enact the plan of killing Riley.

The last throw of the dice: A show of hands

Heading into the hospital room, Mia finds Riley's mother. The pair have a final conversation about how she is part of the family and that it would mean so much if she were to stay there with Riley. This is almost a last moment where Mia would be able to turn back from her mission to kill Riley on which she has set herself. However, it is clear that the addiction to the hand is too strong, and, when Mia is left alone, she sees Riley as one of the entities that she has to destroy.

Meanwhile, Jade arrives at Mia's house and sees the hand and Mia's father, who has been stabbed. She rings to warn her mother, who tells her that Mia has taken Riley. Jade chases after Mia, who is wheeling Riley towards the freeway. Mia then feels the presence of her mother over her shoulder, telling her how proud she is of her and how she is doing the right thing. However, at the last minute, she jumps in front of a moving car without Riley. This mimics the kangaroo at the beginning of the piece.

Act 5: Don't overplay your hand

Mia gets up from the road and suddenly arrives at the hospital. There she sees that Riley is now fine and is ready to go home. All of the lights go out slowly around her, and she cannot see herself in the reflection in the mirror – the fear that she confessed to having in the beginning. She runs screaming after her father saying, 'Don't leave me!' It is clear that he can't hear her, and she gets into the lift. We then cut to black.

There is the striking of a match. Mia follows the lights to find a group of teenagers performing the ritual with a hand of their very own. She reaches for an outstretched hand over a candle. The person on the other end of the ritual says, 'I let you in.' It is now clear that Mia is entirely lost in a dark forest of her own creation.

12

Character Is Structure does TV

One of the questions that we always get asked when we are running a Character Is Structure session in front of an audience is, 'How does this relate to TV?' It is something that we have also considered ourselves, and, as a 'sister' medium to classical narrative cinema, it is true that many of the core ideas we discuss within the book are just as applicable on the small(er) screen as they are on the big(ger) one. Character, after all, remains important as does structure whether your audience is watching your work on an iPhone or an IMAX screen, and, as we have proven, the two are inextricably interlinked. This is particularly true in a modern marketplace where the distance between the definition of film and TV has shrunk and is shrinking further still.

It is a large topic that deserves more time and space than a single chapter, but just to give the burgeoning TV writer in you confidence that everything you have learnt while reading this text also transfers to the creation of the pilot for your next smash-hit show, we will offer some insight here into some of the more nuanced additions that come with writing for TV rather than for film.

Prestige TV

For this chapter, we will be looking explicitly at prestige TV rather than the soaps and serials that take up much of the TV schedules and streaming charts. There has been an explosion of this 'genre' of programming over the past ten years. Akin to the storytelling that we would expect from a well plotted novel, the characters within a prestige TV show should feel as if they are serious people doing serious things that they are taking seriously. Your themes should feel big and important, and the ideas that you are exploring need to be ones that wouldn't look out of place among those winning Emmy Awards. These are the sorts of shows that everyone is watching and that commissioning executives insist they are always looking out for and keen to develop.

Types of pilots

When writing for TV, there are two things that you are probably going to be asked to deliver to showcase that your idea has legs: the first is the pilot script for the first episode, and the second is the 'bible' document that outlines the remainder of the first season and (potentially) beyond. This 'bible' has evolved since the Duffer Brothers created their viral deck for their Netflix smash hit *Stranger Things* (2016) to now be a visual representation of the tone of the show you are creating. For this chapter, though, we will be exclusively focusing on the pilot element of the package you need to produce.

When writing a series, it is a good idea to first frame your work explicitly within one of the four defined types of stories that you want to tell. This will assist you in understanding the channel or streamer that would be most suitable for the idea you are developing and how you might plot the structure and pacing of your narrative.

These four series types are as follows:

1. Perpetual: These ideas run for several seasons and have a story that could go on forever, which is often based around a location or a situation that your characters exist within. These are narratives that we tend not to see outside of soaps, serials or sitcoms and are more suited to a traditional terrestrial TV audience due to the long-running nature of the work. Examples: *Dallas, Tracker, Will Trent*

2. Limited: These are stories that are contained within one season of TV that typically lasts for between six and ten episodes that have the possibility of future seasons on the horizon. This is the sweet spot for

a TV writer and the type of writing that we would encourage you to aim for when crafting a narrative for TV as they allow for a satisfying conclusion after one season but offer you the opportunity to continue to work with the idea moving forward. Examples: *Succession, The White Lotus, Tokyo Vice*

3   Miniseries: A miniseries is one self-contained story that ends with the conclusion of the narrative you are writing within that season of TV. These are typically your big 'event TV' narratives which are more like extended films in their narrative structure and are the pinnacle of prestige TV watching. Examples: *Shōgun, Chernobyl, The Queen's Gambit, The Dropout*

4   Anthology: For an anthology, you are writing a series of shorter, self-contained narratives that have entirely new settings or characters in every episode. They are often linked through tone, theme and genre. Although some incredibly interesting work has come out of anthologies, they are not work we would advise a first-time writer to tackle as they are difficult to develop. Examples: *Inside Number 9, Black Mirror, The Twilight Zone*

Unique elements of TV structure

The first thing to say is that episodic TV is complicated. While we see our story pathways being played out in every series, long-form writing of this type means that these pathways do not generally remain as unbroken narrative threads running through an entire series. An accidental chosen one may morph into a willing chosen one in Episode 3 when they have to retrieve a vital piece of information from an incredibly dangerous situation. An unable-to-believe chosen one may moonlight in Episode 5 as an unknowing chosen one when they do a deal with a peripheral character to fulfil a subplot necessary to the completion of a larger goal. Over a number of hours of storytelling, secondary and tertiary characters become more important, sometimes with whole episodes devoted to their activities; backstory may be delved into in much greater detail than the feature-film writer is used to; and there may even be occasional playful episodes that do not further the central dramatic thread of the piece at all.

We can begin by reassuring you, however, that all of the TV chosen ones start off on one clear pathway. Just like their siblings that you have created for film, they fall distinctively into one of the five paradigms that we have proposed and will be exploring their dark forests using the same elements that we have outlined in this book. However, due to the lengthy nature of the work that you are creating, it may be that they could transition over to another pathway because of the need to sustain the story, or they could intersect with the pathway of another character that alters their response to the story engine.

This will typically happen at a dramaturgically explosive turning point within the narrative arc of a chosen one such as the midpoint or the end of a season (if there are to be additional seasons). John Blackthorne in *Shōgun* begins his narrative journey through feudal Japan as an accidental chosen one as his ship is washed ashore on the island nation. To further compound his status within this paradigm, he even ends up locked away at the bottom of a hole, hoping that he might return home. However, as he climbs his way out and ingratiates himself into Toranaga's favour, he becomes the willing chosen one who is searching for the match that will allow him to burn the forest.

As a note, we have often observed that many of the chosen ones within modern prestige TV seem to always exhibit some elements of the mistaken paradigm. This allows for them to showcase a morality that is a shade of grey and automatically creates a complexity to the character that allows us to debate the decisions that they are making. Grace in *Blue Lights* (2023) is a virtuous and noble chosen one who is clearly on her journey to become a swan. However, she often makes unwise and risky decisions that are away from the typical protocol expected from a police officer serving in Northern Ireland.

Importantly for your pilot, you must reflect the whole of the series within the narrative of the piece. The pilot must be a microcosm of the ideas and themes that you will be exploring as the work continues. There is no point saving a twist or a reveal or a plot point for later down the line … it might be that this is the only bit of writing you ever get to do in this sandbox so make sure that you are stuffing it with all of your most interesting and exciting ideas possible. Always remember that Walter White broke bad in the pilot episode.

With that said, you should always have in the back of your mind how you want the piece to end and ensure that you are steering the work towards this conclusion.

Story engine

When crafting a narrative for TV, you must be certain that the idea you have in mind will sustain the runtime beyond that of a typical film narrative. To do this, you will need to find a story engine that allows you to create an unresolvable conflict and place it at the heart of the show. This story engine will drive the story forward with each episode building on the problem from the pilot. Your story engine will present your chosen one with a monumental problem with which we will watch them wrestling over the ensuing episodes, and we will see how successful, or unsuccessful, they are at holding onto their assumed identity as a result.

In *Breaking Bad* (2008), Walter White is the mild-mannered high school chemistry teacher who collapses one day and receives a cancer diagnosis. Unable to pay his medical bills despite working two jobs, he turns to a life of crime, first producing and then selling methamphetamine to secure the future for himself and his family. However, after accepting this invitation, Walter slowly but surely transitions into his alter ego, Heisenberg, and we in the audience are always left to question how much it is that Walter enjoys his new version of himself as his alter ego allows for the darker elements of his personality to emerge. The story engine that runs the whole series becomes 'Can Walter survive (both physically and spiritually) his life of criminality?' Although there is a simple binary answer to this question, it is also a question that can be revisited and reinvented endlessly, continuing across multiple seasons of TV because of the complexity of Walter's character and the rest of the cast that surround him.

The notion of 'survival' is an interesting one because it invites a never-ending question that can be proposed for your chosen one as there will always be something that threatens them within the narrative world that you have created. Other examples might be:

- Can Beth survive the world of competitive chess while battling addiction? (*The Queen's Gambit*, 2020)
- Will Jake survive the underbelly of Tokyo while reporting on Yakuza activity? (*Tokyo Vice*, 2022)
- How can the heroes of Chernobyl survive one of the worst nuclear disasters in the history of mankind? (*Chernobyl*, 2019)

Multiple plotlines

Although films often do often have several intersecting plotlines that allow for you to explore elements of the narrative away from the central journey of the chosen one, they are all in service of the overarching narrative arc. When writing for TV, it is vital that you are able to showcase different stories within the world that you have created that will sustain and further build on the dramatic tension of the piece. Subordinate characters within the piece must have their own distinct and rich lives within the diegesis you have created so that they can sustain their own dramatic arcs with suitable conclusions. These manifest within your pilot as the B, C and possibly D stories that allow for other characters to influence and/or showcase their own special status. Each of these characters will probably be on their own specific pathway that allows you to explore their reactions to the invitation through a different lens.

In narratives focusing on single protagonists, the A story within the pilot will typically be exclusively about the chosen one and allow us to see what their archetypal response to the story engine will be. It will settle the audience into the rhythm of the show and allow them to understand the trajectory that they will be on during the run of the show. The B story will be a key dramatic element that will develop on a recurring component of the broader mythology of the piece. We will see a love interest blossom, how a key ally will assist the chosen one, or explore the backstory or motivations of the chosen one. The C story will do these things but typically involve an additional character or characters who is/are much more at the fringes of the immediate set of core characters that are involved with the central narrative of the show. Alternatively, it might be that you can explore the relationships between two recurring characters who will come more to the forefront of the narrative later on. Imagine the A story of the piece as you zooming out on the plot of the story with you zooming into some of the more intimate moments of your story as you progress into the B and C strands of your narrative.

For example, in *Ozark* (2017), Marty Byrde is a willing chosen one who has to try and make enough money for the cartel so that he is able to survive in this new world of criminality within which he finds himself. As a skilled accountant, he has the physical abilities to be able to complete this task; however, he (at least initially) has to wrestle with the moral implications of what he must do. The other characters in his family, and the surrogate family that he begins to surround himself with in the first season, are each on their own pathway that require him to deviate from his initial path on occasion. His wife Laura initially enters into a deal with him so that they will play happy families in order to assist him in completing his task. After all, her life is just as much in danger as his. Marty's son, Jonah, is desperately looking for a mentor figure to assist him through this tumultuous time in his life and is therefore on an unable-to-believe pathway. Charlotte, the daughter of the Byrde family, has merely fallen down a rabbit hole into this life and is simply looking to go home. When these families intersect with Marty's pathway in a B or C plot, it requires him to adjust his trajectory and engage with them to assist them in discovering the answer to the central dramatic situation in which they find themselves.

Two invitations

In writing for TV, you explicitly explore your chosen one's central dilemma by offering two different invitations within your pilot episode. The first is the invitation to the pilot. This invitation will end the status quo for our chosen one's once upon a time and will take our chosen one from Act 1 into Act 2. In *Breaking Bad*, this is the moment when Walter White collapses and finally understands that he has cancer. In *Succession* (2018), this is when Kendall Roy is trying to save the floundering deal that he is overseeing during the pilot, something that his father is very keen for him to get right.

The second invitation to the series typically happens as we transition from Act 4 into Act 5. This moment ensures that your chosen one is never able to return to their status quo and reinforces the story engine that will help to progress the series. This is a moment that should ensure your audience has to come back and, in its most effective form, will hint at the broader conflicted nature of your chosen one. In *Succession* this is where Logan Roy collapses in the helicopter and the family are now thrown into the turmoil of working out who will succeed the ageing media mogul. With *Breaking Bad*, Walter has survived his initial encounter with the world of methamphetamine and really begins to question his identity as he fishes the money out of his tumble dryer. Tellingly, as he gets into bed as the episode ends, his wife asks him, 'Walter, is that you?' In both of these cases, it is clear that the writer(s) know precisely where this series is heading.

Leveraging the point of view of your chosen one

When considering how you are going to write your pilot, always be considering what is the point of view (POV) of your pilot and how do you leverage this to gain the greatest number of dramatic situations from it? Typically, TV will fall into three distinct types of POV that would allow you to explore the central conflict of the narrative in a coherent way: (1) single chosen one; (2) dual chosen ones; and (3) ensemble of chosen ones. The simplest way to unpack this is through the duality of the chosen one(s) that we have within the narrative you have created. In this we can see the contrasting or contradictory responses to the story engine that you have established within the pilot episode.

Single-chosen-one shows

For a single-chosen-one show, you will explore the story engine through one dominant perspective. This is the type of narrative that allows for rich and engaging character studies where the duality of a chosen one is explored within them. This limited POV is particularly important because the series lead typically has something to hide, and how and when you reveal this secret to the other characters is a great way to draw out the tension and drama. Often the hidden half of the chosen one sits within the mistaken paradigm so that we are able to see the constructive and destructive sides of their personality.

For example, in *Barry* (2018), Barry is a hitman who discovers the joy of acting while he is out looking for his next target. However, these two worlds cannot coexist, and Barry is frequently seeing them collide with disastrous results as it becomes increasingly hard to juggle rehearsals and the contract killings that he must go through with. He straddles the mistaken and unable-to-believe paradigms. He has two specific (tor)mentor figures in Gene Cousineau and Monroe Fuches who are pulling/pushing him further and further down the respective paths they are trying to assist him in navigating, and it is up to Barry to try and navigate their respective demands as best he can.

Dual-chosen-ones shows

With a pilot with two very clear chosen ones, the duality is between them. During the narrative, the POV shifts between the two distinctive responses to the story engine so that an audience can understand the perspectives that the chosen ones have. Dual-chosen-one shows are almost always improved and enhanced when each of the equal chosen ones have very different ideas about how they will solve the central problem that you are placing in their path.

A great example of this is *The English* (2022), set in the 1890s, when an Englishwoman called Cornelia Locke travels to the American West to seek revenge on the man she sees as responsible for the death of her son. Although she appears determined and resilient, she is not cut out for the world that she finds in America and is something of an accidental chosen one who finds herself swept up in a narrative that, at the beginning, she has no control over. During her journey, she meets Eli Whipp who has recently left the US Army and is looking to settle down on the land he has been promised because of his service. Cornelia and Eli make a deal that throws him headfirst into an unknowing arc that will have him explore his response to the agreement they made and his responsibility for her as they adventure through the West. It is testament to the brilliant writing of Hugo Blick that the importance of this central relationship is so well crafted but also outlined to us within the opening monologue from Cornelia. Once again, the writer is clearly aware of the end of his series as he writes the beginning.

Ensemble-chosen-ones shows

If you are writing a show with an ensemble of chosen ones, the duality is mainly between our cast of characters and the dark forest you have developed. The dark forest or location of your drama becomes the final chosen one, and the conflict is how our chosen ones do (or more than likely do not) fit into it, and how the team that you have created within the narrative works together to solve the question that the story engine throws at them adds to the conflict. This is obviously informed by the various conflicted natures that they exhibit and their growing relationships. In ensemble shows, several characters might be involved in the same A, B, or even C story and are able to represent different archetypal figures to one another. Each subsequent episode after the pilot allows you to develop the dominant POV of the A story so that the audience is able to learn something new about the cast and the relationships that they have with one another.

Halt and Catch Fire (2014) is an ensemble show set during the personal-computer revolution of the late 1980s and early 1990s. Each of our chosen ones is a maverick in their own right, and the story becomes how they will be able to survive as they work together within the dark forest which continues to grow in scope and size. Each of them enters and leaves the lives of the other for a period of time and allows for other characters to enter their orbit which helps change their response to the initial story engine that appeared in the pilot episode.

Conclusions

As previously mentioned, TV is a complex subject in its own right, and it would take much more time than outlined here to fully explore the subtleties of an art form that is adjacent to writing for film. There are, however, always certain truisms no matter the medium you are working in when telling stories: character *is* structure; simple plot, complex characters; and audiences enjoy watching active progress through a narrative.

Remember: people want to be told a story, and all the tools in this and our previous book are given to you in the hopes that they will help you to tell your stories in the most effective, most dramatic, most enjoyable and, crucially, most original way. We are not in the business of creating templates for cookie-cutter narratives. Our aim is to give you the means to form your narratives and shape your storylines so that they touch your audience and deliver the shocks, laughs, emotions and dramas that every well-told tale should have embedded within them.

We often deliver talks and presentations to writers struggling with their material, and some of the most common questions revolve around the angst and pain that some writers feel in the development of their work. Our response is always the same. You're not enjoying it enough. If you're not enjoying it, stop doing it. Play with the words and the images and the characters within the parameters we have provided for you, and hopefully you will find an arena that will remind you why you decided to write this thing in the first place. Writing is a joyful activity and should always be done with that thought in mind. Enjoy yourselves.

Index

A Bug's Life (1999) 19, 28
Abdullah, Ahmed 36, 38
accidental chosen one xviii, xxi, xxiv; 11–13, 14, 63–77, 135–148, 163, 167 *see also Everything Everywhere All at Once*; gatekeeper; *Wizard of Oz, The*
accidental storyline xviii; 11, 63, 64, 65, 66, 67, 68, 69, 70, 71, 72, 73, 74, 75, 76, 77, 140, 146, 148
acts xviii–xix, 22, 23, 26, 28, 31, 32, 45, 71, 95, 97, 99, 102, 103, 105, 108, 113, 116, 117, 118, 123, 126, 128, 130, 131, 134. 137, 141, 143, 144, 147, 152, 155, 158, 160, 167, 168
    Act 1 xix, 27, 31, 39, 40, 95–97, 108–111, 123–125, 136–139, 151–152, 167
    Act 2 xix, 97–99, 111- 113, 126–128, 137–141, 152–155, 167
    Act 3 xix, 99–102, 113–116, 128–131, 141–143, 155–158, 167
    Act 4 xix, 103–104, 117–118, 131–133, 144–146, 158–159, 168
    Act 5 xix, 29, 105, 118, 134, 147, 160, 168
    five-act model xix, 104, 144
addiction 150, 155, 157, 159, 166
adventure xix, xx, 19, 21, 32, 33, 67, 77, 151, 152
Afghanistan 36, 37, 38, 40, 41, 42, 44
Agent Smith 11
Alan (Barbie character) 124, 131
Aliena (fictional character) 109, 114
allegory 93

allies 26, 27, 30, 32
Alpha Gong Gong 142, 143, 147
Alpha Waymond 137, 138, 140, 142, 143, 145, 147
American Fiction (2023) 80, 82, 87, 91
Any Given Sunday (1999) 60
Anxiety (Inside Out 2 character) 21, 93, 94, 98, 99, 100, 101, 102, 103, 104, 105
anti-hero x, xviii, 13, 79
Avatar (2009) 24
Autopsy of Jane Doe, The (2016) 81

Baby Reindeer (2024) 77
Back to the Future (1985) 64, 65, 66, 68, 72, 73, 74, 135, 136
backstory 28, 80, 163, 166
bagel 141, 145, 146, 147
Barbie (2023) vii, 121–134
    Barbie (character) 121, 122, 123, 124, 125, 126, 127, 128, 129, 130, 131, 132, 133, 134
    Barbie Land 123, 124, 126, 127, 130, 131, 133
bargain xvii, 35, 37, 39, 41, 108, 109, 155
Barry (2018) 169
basket xv, xvi, xxii
Bass, Saul 78
Baumbach, Noah 121, 122
Beaubeirdre, Deidre 137, 138, 148
Becky (Everything Everywhere character) 136, 148
Becky (Fall character) 4.50
belief 8, 9, 27, 50, 51, 54, 55, 60, 69, 82, 95, 96, 99, 100, 101, 103, 104, 105, 125, 126, 131

Belief System (*Inside Out 2*) 95, 96, 99, 101, 103, 105
Bertie (*The King's Speech*) 52, 54, 131
BFI (British Film Institute)iv
bible (TV writing) 162
Big (1988) 64, 65, 67, 68, 69, 73, 74, 75, 76
Billy (*Big*) 67, 76
Birds of Prey (2020) C 23
BlacKkKlansman (2018) 47
Blue Lights (2023) 164
Blunt, Emily 107
Bond, James 78
Bree (*Inside Out 2* character) 95, 99
Brody (*Jaws*) 22
Brothers Grimm xvi, xxi
Brynn (*No One Will Save You*) 80, 82, 84
Buffalo Bill 37, 38, 44
Byrde, Marty 167

Cage, Nicolas 37
Cain, Cassandra 23
Character Is Structure x, 161 *see also* Simple story, complex character
   archetypes 166, 170
   complexity xii, xiv, xv, 17, 2, 5, 7, 20, 39, 69, 82, 87, 149, 164, 171
   conflicted nature xix, 11, 17, 27, 45, 55, 64, 74, 81, 93, 104, 149, 150, 168
   development x, 5, 27, 50, 82, 150, 171,
Chernobyl (2019) 163, 166
chosen one x, xiii, xv–xix, xxi, xxii, xxiii, xxiv, 1–17, 19–33, 35–46, 49–62, 63–77, 79–92, 93, 95, 96, 97, 99, 101, 104, 107, 109, 110, 111, 113, 115, 116, 117, 119, 121, 123, 124, 125, 126, 128, 129, 130, 131, 132, 135, 136, 137, 138, 139, 140, 141, 142, 143, 144, 145, 146, 148, 149, 150, 151, 152, 153, 154, 155, 156, 157, 158, 159, 163, 164, 165, 166, 167, 168, 169, 170
   accidental xviii, xxi, xxiv, 11–13, 14, 63–77, 135–148, 163, 167
   dual chosen ones 168, 169–170

ensemble chosen ones 168, 170
mistaken xviii, xxiv, 13–15, 79–92, 149–160, 164, 169
single chosen one 168–169
unable-to-believe xvii, xxiv, 8–11, 14, 49–62, 121–134, 163, 167, 169
unknowing xvii, xxii, xxiv, 5–8, 14, 35–48, 107–119, 163, 167, 169, 170
willing xvii, xxi, xxiv, 2–5, 14, 19–33, 93–105, 164, 167
Cinderella xv, 125
Citadel (*Furiosa*) 70
Coach Roberts 95
Cole (*Talk to Me*) 150
Comanche 29
conflict xiii, xiv, 20, 21, 26, 94, 98, 145, 151, 165, 168
Connors, Phil 135, 136
console (*Inside Out 2*) 95, 96, 97, 98, 99, 100, 101, 102, 103, 104, 105
Covenant, The (2023) 36, 37, 38, 40, 42
Cowardly Lion 69, 140
Crawl (2019) 13
Crawford (Agent) 37, 38, 44
Cuarón, Alfonso CH5.75

Dallas 162
dark forest x, xi, xiii, xiv, xvii, xix, xx, xxi, xxii, xxiii, xxiv, 1, 2, 3, 4, 5, 6, 7, 8, 9, 11, 13, 14, 15, 20, 21, 22, 24, 25, 26, 27, 28, 30, 31, 32, 35, 36, 37, 40, 45, 46, 50, 51, 52, 54, 63, 64, 66, 68, 69, 71, 72, 73, 74, 79, 80, 81, 82, 83, 85, 86, 87, 88, 89, 90, 91, 92, 97, 99, 105, 109, 111, 113, 126, 131, 136, 137, 138, 139, 140, 141, 142, 143, 144, 148, 152, 153, 155, 157, 158, 160, 164, 169, 170
Darth Vader xiii, 29
deal xvii, 5, 6, 7, 35, 36, 37, 38, 39, 41, 45, 79, 80, 108, 109, 111, 112, 113, 115, 119, 163, 167
Debbie (*The Searchers*) 29
Decision to Leave (2022) 80, 84, 87
Delroy, Jack 87, 90

Dementus 70
Dementors 136
Desmond, Norma 80
Devil Wears Prada, The (2006) 8
Die Hard (1988) 63, 65, 67, 68, 69, 71, 74, 76, 136
disruptor xvii, 6, 35, 36, 39, 42, 45, 43
Docter, Pete 93
Doolittle, Eliza 51, 53, 54, 131
Doone (*The Fall Guy* character) 112, 113
Dorothy (*Wizard of Oz*) 65, 67, 68, 69, 71, 73, 74, 76, 139, 140, 146
Doug (*The Hangover*) 23
Dwayne (*Little Miss Sunshine*) 56
Dropout, The 163
Dumb Money (2023) 24, 25, 26, 27, 28
Dumbledore, Albus 53
Dune: Part Two (2024) xvii
Durden, Tyler 53, 54, 58

Edwards, Ethan 29
Ego, Anton 94
Ellison, Thelonious 'Monk' 80
Elsa (*Jojo Rabbit*) 35, 110
Emerald City 65, 68, 139, 140
Emotions (*Inside Out 2*) 21, 93, 94, 95, 96, 97, 98, 99, 100, 101, 102, 103, 104, 105
End We Start From, The (2023) xviii, 65
English, The (2022) 169
Ennui (Inside Out 2 character) 98, 101, 102
Everdeen, Katniss 24, 26
Evil Dead Rise (2023) xviii

fairy tales xiv, xv, xxi, 2, 63, 76, 125
Fall (2022) 50
Farquaad, Lord 110
Fast and the Furious, The 107
Fight Club (1999) 53, 54, 58
Final Girl 89
Fleabag (2016) 77
Fletcher, Terence 53
folk tales xiv, 11
Force, The 29

Foxcatcher (2014) 53
Frank (*Little Miss Sunshine*) 56
Frodo Baggins 23
Fun with Dick and Jane (2005) 46
Furiosa: A Mad Max Saga (2024) 70

Gail Meyer 108, 109, 110, 113, 114, 116, 117, 118
Gamestop 27
gate xx, xxi, xxii, xxiii, xxiv, 1, 2, 6, 7, 9, 10, 11, 12, 14, 25, 28, 36, 37, 38, 39, 40, 45, 54, 56, 57, 58, 59, 62, 65, 66, 67, 68, 69, 71, 72, 73, 88, 89, 90, 97, 104, 111, 112, 115, 117, 125, 139, 140, 142, 143, 145, 146, 148, 153, 157, 164
  first gate xxi, 6, 7, 36, 37, 38, 39, 40, 42, 43, 45, 115, 116
  second gate xxi, 6, 36, 37, 39, 40, 45, 109, 117
  gatekeeper xxi, 12, 13, 65, 66, 67, 68, 69, 70, 71, 72, 73, 74, 77, 143, 144, 148
genre xxi, 16, 11, 59, 69, 77, 82, 151, 163, 170
George (*Back to the Future*) 66, 69, 72, 73, 74, 110
Gerwig, Greta 121, 122, 140
Gill, Keith (Roaring Kitty) 25, 27, 28
Gillis, Joe 80, 85, 88
Gloria (*Barbie*) 127, 129, 130, 131, 132, 133
Godfather, The (1972) 82, 83, 84
Godzilla Minus One (2023) 24, 25
Gollum 23
Gong Gong 136, 137, 138, 142, 143, 147
Gosling, Ryan 107
Grace (Inside Out 2 character) 95, 99, 104, 105
Grandma/grandmother xv, xvi, xxii, xxiii, 2, 5, 7, 8, 9, 10, 4
Gravity (2013) 64, 65, 67, 69, 70, 72, 74, 75
Green Book (2019) 56
Groundhog Day (1993) 135, 136, 139

Gruber, Hans 68, 69, 71, 74
Guardians of the Galaxy Vol. 2 (2017) xvii
Gumb, Jame 38, 41, 42

Hae-jun, Jang 80, 87
Halt and Catch Fire (2014) 170
Hannay, Richard 64
Hard Candy (2005) 5
Harley Quinn 23
Harker, 83
Harry Potter and the Prisoner of Azkaban (2004) 136
Harry Potter and the Philosopher's Stone (2001) 53
Hayley (*Talk to Me*) 151, 152, 154, 155
Headquarters (Inside Out 2) 21, 95, 96, 97, 98, 99, 100, 101, 103, 105
Heisenberg 165
Help (2021) 25, 27, 29
Henderson, Iris 64
Henry (*The Fall Guy*) 115, 116, 117
Higgins, Henry 51, 53
Hitchcock, Alfred 64, 78
Holstein, Dave 93
Holdovers, The (2023) xvii
Holly McClane 63, 68, 71
Hooper (*Jaws*) CH2.22
horror xviii, 15, 79, 80, 82, 84, 150, 151, 154
Hoover, Olive 55, 58
Howie, Neil 15
Hunt, Ethan 26
Hunger Games, The (2012) 24
Hunter (*Fall*) 50
huntsman xv, xxi, xxii, xxiii, 2, 3, 4, 6, 7, 8, 9, 12, 13, 14

I Saw the TV Glow (2024) xviii, 80, 91
Iggy Starr 112
IMAX 161
Inception (2010) 135
Indiana Jones and The Last Crusade (1989) 23
Inside Number 9 163
Inside Out (2015) 93

Inside Out 2 (2024) vii, 21, 93–105
Instigators, The (2024) xvii
Interstellar (2014) 135
invitation x, xvii, xix, 5, 9, 14, 21, 22, 35, 36, 37, 41, 46, 51, 52, 64, 77, 79, 81, 82, 83, 85, 88, 90, 96, 109, 110, 111, 123, 124, 125, 138, 151, 152, 165, 167, 168

Jade (*Talk to Me*) 151, 152, 153, 154, 157, 158, 160
Jaiyah Saelua 59
Japan 16, 24, 29, 164
Jaws (1975) 22
Jeff (*Hard Candy*) 5
Jedi xiii, xiv, 28, 29
Jojo Rabbit (2019) 35, 36, 110
Jonah Byrde 167
Joss (*Talk to Me*) 152, 155
Joy (Inside Out 2 character) 21, 93, 94, 95, 96, 97, 98, 99, 100, 101, 102, 103, 104, 105
Joy Wang 136, 137, 138, 141, 143, 145, 147, 148

Kaplan, George 64, 66, 68, 69
Karate Kid, The (1984) 51, 52, 53, 54, 55, 58, 60, 131
Ken (Barbie character) 123, 124, 125, 126, 127, 128, 130, 132, 133
Kendall Roy 167
key xx, xxi, xxii, xxiii, xxiv, 1, 7, 9, 10, 11, 14, 22, 27, 39, 40, 45, 53, 58, 59, 65, 71, 73, 90, 97, 109, 111, 117, 125, 140, 141, 145, 148, 153
Kinley, John 36, 37, 38, 39, 40, 41, 42, 44
King's Speech, The (2010) 52, 53, 54, 57
Koichi Shikishima 24, 25
Korpi, Aatami xvii
Kora (*Rebel Moon*) 28, 30, 31
Kowalski (*Gravity*) 67, 70, 73, 75
Kreese, Sensei 51
Kross (*Pretty Woman*) 41, 43
Kurosawa, Akira 19, 20

Lamb (2021) 82
Land of Bad (2024) xviii
LaRusso, Daniel 51, 52, 53, 54, 57, 58
last throw of the dice x, xix, 26, 28, 37, 11, 50, 82, 104, 118, 133, 146
Lawrence, Johnny 51, 57
Lawrence of Arabia (1962) 16
Lecter, Hannibal 37, 38, 41, 42, 44
LeFauve, Meg 93
Lego Movie, The (2014) 24, 121
Lehman, Ernest 66
Lewis, Edward (*Pretty Woman*) 38, 40, 41, 43, 44, 110
Lifeboat (1944) 64
Lilly (*Late Night with the Devil*) 87, 90
Little Miss Sunshine (2006) 49, 55, 56, 58
Little Red Riding Hood xv, xvi, xxi, xxii, xxiii, xxiv, 1, 2, 5, 6, 7, 8, 9, 10, 11, 12, 13, 14
Locke, Cornelia 169, 170
Logue, Lionel 52, 53, 57
Longlegs (2024) 81, 83
London Screenwriters' Festival ix
Lorraine McFly 66, 72
Lord of the Rings: The Fellowship of the Ring (2001) 49
Lord of the Rings: The Return of the King (2003) 23
Lots-o'-Huggin' 94
Luke Skywalker xii, xiii, 29, 51

MacGuffin 22
Maddy (*I Saw the TV Glow*) 80, 91
Mad Max Saga 70
Magnificent Seven, The (1961) 19
Mann, Kelsey 93
March-Phillips, Gus xvii
Master, The (2012) 47
match xxi, 3, 4, 5, 22–26, 28, 97, 100
Matrix, The (1999) 10, 60, 136
Maude (*No One Will Save You*) 82
McClane, John 63, 65, 67, 68, 69, 71, 74, 76
McFly, Marty 65, 66, 69, 70, 72, 73, 76; CH10.136

Meet the Parents (2000) 47
Men in Black (1997) 22
mentor xvii, xxi, 8, 9, 10, 49, 50, 51, 52, 53, 54, 55, 56, 57, 58, 59, 60, 80, 124, 125, 129, 132, 133, 167, 169
mentor/tormentor xxi, 49, 50, 51, 52, 53, 54, 55, 56, 57, 58, 169
Menu, The (2022) 79, 82, 88
Metalstorm (fictional film) 108, 109, 112, 113, 114, 115, 117, 118
Mia (*Talk to Me*) 149, 150, 151, 152, 153, 154, 155, 156, 157, 158, 159, 160
midpoint x, xix, 17, 4, 71, 101, 115, 129, 142, 143, 156, 164, 167
Milan, Alma 114
Miller, Captain (*Saving Private Ryan*) 31
Ministry of Ungentlemanly Warfare, The (2024) xvii
Mission Impossible: Rogue Nation (2015) 111
mistaken/accidental xviii, 15, 80, 81, 84, 151
mistaken/unable-to-believe xviii, 14, 80
mistaken/unknowing xviii, 14, 79
mistaken/willing xviii, 14, 80
Miyagi, Mr 51, 52, 53, 57, 58
Mojo Dojo Casa House 130, 132
monologue 28, .57, 90,101, 116, 118, 130, 131, 132, 170
Morpheus 10, 11
multiverse 135, 139, 141, 142, 143, 144, 145, 146, 147, 148
My Fair Lady 51, 53, 54, 55
My Pafology (fictional book) 82
My Small Land (2022) 16

Nakatomi Plaza 65, 67, 68, 71
narrative Intro.x, xi, xiii, xiv, xv, xvii, xix; CH1.2, 4, 5, 6, 14, 15, 17; CH2.19, 20, 21, 22, 23, Neo 10, 11, 60
Next Goal Wins (2023) 59
Noble, Atticus 28
Nolan, Christopher 78, 135
No One Will Save You (2023) 80, 82, 85
North by Northwest (1959) 64, 66, 68, 69, 70, 72, 74, 75, 76

Obi-Wan Kenobi 51
off the path xx, xxi, xxiii, xxiv, 1, 3, 7, 14, 26–28, 40–41, 42, 43, 46, 55–57, 71–74, 85–87, 97, 111, 125, 141, 142, 152, 153, 155, 158, 166
One Life (2023) xvii
Orion's Belt 22
Owen (*I Saw the TV Glow*) 80, 91
Ozark (2017) 167

Palahniuk, Chuck 59
Panem 24
Parasite (2023) 85
Parker (*The Covenant*) 41
path xix, xx, xxi, xxii, xxiii, xxiv, 1, 3, 6, 7, 8, 9, 11, 12, 13, 14, 22, 25, 26, 28, 30, 31, 35, 36, 37, 38, 39, 40, 41, 42, 43, 45, 46, 50, 51, 52, 54, 55, 56, 57, 59, 65, 66, 68, 69, 70, 71, 72, 84, 85, 86, 88, 97, 110, 111, 112, 113, 115, 125, 126, 127, 128, 130, 131, 132, 139, 140, 141, 142, 148, 150, 152, 153, 155, 158, 167, 169
pathway x, xvi, xvii, xix, xxi, xxiv, 1, 2, 5, 6, 7, 8, 11, 12, 13, 14, 19, 21, 22, 25, 33, 35, 36, 37, 39, 45, 46, 50, 65, 74, 76 ,79, 83, 163, 164, 166, 167
Pearce, Drew 107, 111, 112
Pendleton Hotel 112, 115
Perrault, Charles xvi, 11
Phantom Menace, The (1999) xiv
Philip (*Pretty Woman*) 43
Philippou, Danny 149
pilot (TV) 161, 162, 163, 164, 165, 166, 167, 168, 169, 170
Pixar 31, 93
plot xiii, 17, 27, 48, 65, 94, 109, 110, 112, 115, 122, 150, 162, 164, 166, 167, 171
pod-racing xiv
Potter, Mr 46
Pouchy 99, 104
Powell, Al 67, 68, 69
Pretty Woman (1990) 37, 38, 40, 43; CH8.110

Priestly, Miranda 8
protagonist xiv, xv, 5, 14, 158, 166

Queen's Gambit, The 163, 166
question xi, xii, xiv, 16, 17, 17, 20, 21, 22, 27, 28, 36, 39, 50, 61, 65, 81, 82, 84, 90, 94, 95, 96, 98, 101, 110, 114, 129, 139, 143, 150, 152, 165, 171
Quick, Oliver 90
Quiet Girl, The (2022) xviii
Quint (*Jaws*) 22

Rapunzel xv
Ratatouille (2007) 94
Rebel Moon (2023) 19, 28, 30, 31
Rebel Moon - Part Two: The Scargiver (2024) 30
Reiko Asakawa 80
Riley (*Inside Out 2*) 21, 27, 93, 95, 96, 97, 98, 99, 100, 101, 102, 103, 104, 105
Riley (*Talk to Me*) 151, 152, 153, 154, 155, 156, 158, 159, 160
Ring (1998) 80, 85, 86
Ritchie, Guy 36
road movie 49, 56, 57
Rocky (1967) 53
Rongen, Thomas 59, 60
Ron Kay 41
Rose (*Smile*) 80, 84, 88
Ruth Handler 129, 133, 134
Ryder, Tom 108, 109, 110, 111, 112, 113, 114, 115, 116, 117, 118

Sadako 85, 86
Sadness (Inside Out 2 character) 95, 96, 98, 100, 101, 102, 103
Saelua, Jaiyah 59
Sally (*Texas Chainsaw Massacre*) 16
Saltburn (2023) xviii, 90
Sarah (*Help*) 25, 27, 29
Sarya (*My Small Land*) 16
Sasha (*Barbie*) 128, 129, 130, 131, 132, 133
Saving Private Ryan (1998) 23, 31
Scarecrow 69, 73, 140
Scream xi

Seavers, Colt 108, 109, 110, 111, 112, 113, 114, 115, 116, 117, 118, 119
Seo-rae, Song 80, 84, 87
Seven Samurai (1954) xi, 19, 29
Shane (1953) 29
Shirley, Don 56
Shōgun 163, 164
Shrek (2001) 110
Silence of the Lambs, The (1991) xi, 37, 38, 40, 42
simple story, complex character xii, xiv, 17, 2, 149, 171
sin 81, 82, 83, 84, 85, 86, 87, 150, 152, 154
Sisu (2022) xvii
Slowik, Julian 82, 88
Sleeping Beauty xiv, xv
Smile (2022) 80, 81, 82, 84, 88, 91
Smith, Agent 11
Soul (2021) 139
Space Cowboy (fictional character) 109, 114
Stanton, Andrew 16
Starling, Clarice 37, 38, 40, 41, 42, 44
Star Wars xi, xii, xiv, 51
  Star Wars: Episode I - The Phantom Menace xiv
  Star Wars: Episode IV - A New Hope xi, xii, 51
  Star Wars: Episode VI - Return of the Jedi 28, 29
stakes xiv, 21, 23, 24, 94, 100, 110, 151, 153
Stone, Dr Ryan 65, 67, 70, 72, 73, 75, 76
story engine 165, 166, 167, 168, 170
Stranger Things (2016) 162
structure x, vii, ix, 17, 20, 50, 51, 53, 59, 104, 121, 144, 161, 162, 163, 166, 171
Sturges, John 19
subplot 56, 100, 125, 163
subtext 60, 61, 65, 153, 166
Succession (2018) 163, 167, 168
suit of armour xx, xxi, xxii, xxiv, 1, 3, 7, 9, 13, 14, 20, 31–32, 43–45, 54, 75–76, 87–89, 97, 111, 112, 115, 117, 119, 125, 141, 148, 152

Summerisle 15
Sunset Boulevard (1950) 80, 85, 88
Susan (*Big*) 67
Swan, Edith xviii
swan xvii, 8, 10, 14, 50, 51, 60, 80, 164
Swift, Taylor 107

Taliban 38, 40, 41, 42, 44
Talk to Me (2023) vii, 82, 83, 149–160
TED Talk 16
Tenet (2020) 135
Terminator (1984) 135
Texas Chainsaw Massacre, The (1974) 16, 84
theme(s) ix, 20, 31, 51, 75, 122, 149, 150, 162, 163, 164, 171
39 Steps, The (1935) 64
Thornhill, Roger 64, 66, 68, 69, 70, 72, 76
Thoroughbreds (2017) 89
Tin Man 69, 73, 140
Tokyo Vice 163, 166
tone 11, 17, 20, 24, 33, 49, 51, 59, 78, 80, 94, 150, 154, 162, 163, 170
Tony (*Help*) CH2.27
Tony Lip 56
Toranaga 164
tormentor xvii, xxi, 8, 9, 49, 50, 51, 52, 53, 54, 55, 56, 57, 58, 59, 60, 80, 169
Toy Story 3 (2010) 94
Tracker 162
Trading Places (1983) 46
trauma 59, 82, 147, 150
treatment xiii
tropes 5, 24, 149
Tucker, Dan 108, 115, 116
TV vii, ix, 50, 149, 161–171
  anthology 163
  limited series 162
  miniseries 163
  perpetual series 162
  pilot 161, 162, 163, 164, 165, 166, 167, 168
  prestige 161, 163, 164
Twilight Zone, The 163
Tyler (*The Menu*) 79, 82, 88

unable-to-believe chosen one xvii, xxiv, 8–11, 14, 49–62, 121–134, 163, 167, 169
unknowing chosen one xvii, xxii, xxiv, 5–8, 14, 35–48, 107–119, 163, 167, 169, 170
Unbearable Weight of Massive Talent, The (2022) 37
Unobtainium 24

Val (Valentina) 97, 98, 99, 100, 101
Vandamm, Phillip 69, 75
Veldt (*Rebel Moon*) 19
Veneziano, Gabriele 135
verse jumping 139, 140, 145

Waititi, Taika 8
Evelyn Wang 136, 137, 138, 139, 140, 141, 142, 143, 144, 145, 146, 147, 148
Wang, Waymond 136, 137, 138, 140, 141, 145, 147, 148
Ward, Vivian 38, 40, 41, 43, 44, 45, 110
Wayne, John 29

Whale, The (2022) xvii
Wicker Man, The (1973) 15
Wicked Little Letters (2023) xviii
Wicked Witch of the West 67, 68, 69, 71, 74, 140
Will Trent 162
willing chosen one xvii, xxi, xxiv, 2–5, 14, 19–33, 93–105, 164, 167
Willis, Bruce 63
Wizard of Oz, The xi, 63, 64, 68, 69, 71, 74, 139, 146
wolf xx, xxi, xxii, xxiii, xxiv, 1, 2, 3, 4, 5, 6, 7, 8, 9, 10, 11, 12, 13, 14, 20, 22, 28, 30–31, 36, 41–43, 45, 51, 59, 65, 69, 71, 74–75, .80, 82, 83–85, 88, 89, 90, 92, 93, 97, 109, 111, 116, 119, 125, 138, 141, 145, 148, 152, 153, 155

Yōichi 86

Zemeckis, Robert 135
Zimmerman, Flip 47
Zoltar machine 65, 73, 76